EXPLORE

LAS VEGAS

YOUR FREE EBOOK AVAILABLE THROUGH THE WALKING EYE APP

Your guide now includes a free eBook to your chosen destination, for the same great price as before. Simply download the Walking Eye App from the App Store or Google Play to access your free eBook.

HOW THE WALKING EYE APP WORKS

Through the Walking Eye App, you can purchase a range of eBooks and destination content. However, when you buy this book, you can download the corresponding eBook for free. Just see below in the grey panel where to find your free content and then scan the QR code at the bottom of this page.

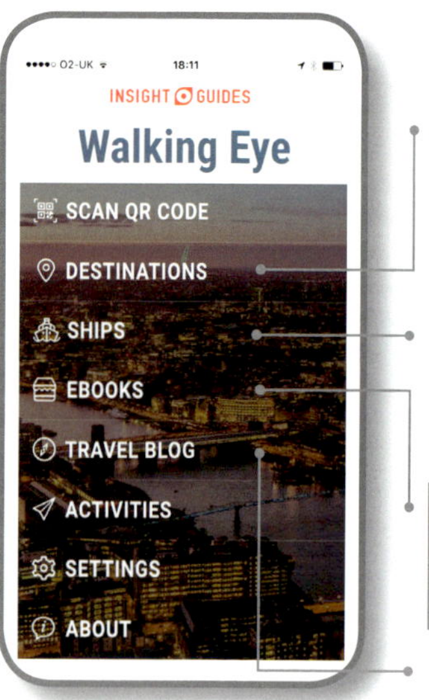

Destinations: Download essential destination content featuring recommended sights and attractions, restaurants, hotels and an A–Z of practical information, all available for purchase.

Ships: Interested in ship reviews? Find independent reviews of river and ocean ships in this section, all available for purchase.

eBooks: You can download your free accompanying digital version of this guide here. You will also find a whole range of other eBooks, all available for purchase.

Free access to travel-related blog articles about different destinations, updated on a daily basis.

HOW THE EBOOKS WORK

The eBooks are provided in EPUB file format. Please note that you will need an eBook reader installed on your device to open the file. Many devices come with this as standard, but you may still need to install one manually from Google Play.

The eBook content is identical to the content in the printed guide.

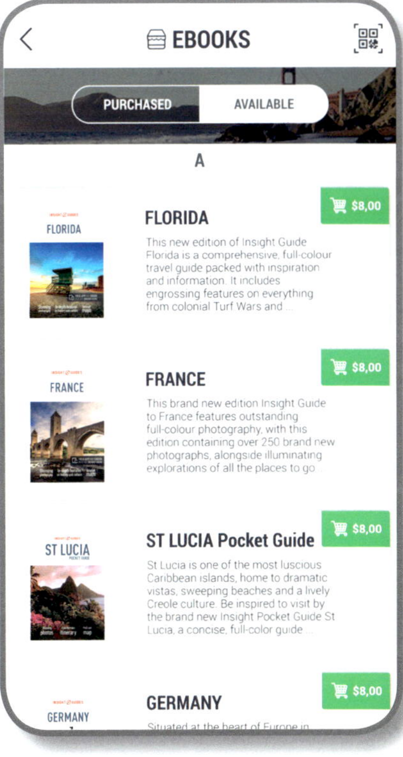

HOW TO DOWNLOAD THE WALKING EYE APP

1. Download the Walking Eye App from the App Store or Google Play.
2. Open the app and select the scanning function from the main menu.
3. Scan the QR code on this page – you will then be asked a security question to verify ownership of the book.
4. Once this has been verified, you will see your eBook in the purchased ebook section, where you will be able to download it.

Other destination apps and eBooks are available for purchase separately or are free with the purchase of the Insight Guide book.

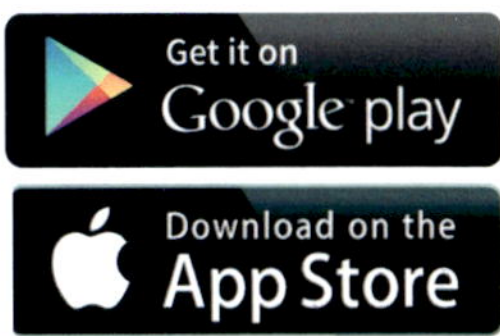

VEGAS

POKER

CONTENTS

Introduction

Recommended Routes for... 6
Explore Las Vegas 10
Food and Drink 16
Shopping 18
Gambling 20
Weddings 22
History: Key Dates 24

Directory

Accommodations 84
Restaurants 94
Nightlife 104
A–Z 110
Books and Film 122

Credits

About This Book 124
Credits 125
Index 126

Best Routes

1. Classic Las Vegas 28
2. All-natural Vegas 32
3. Artistic Las Vegas 36
4. International Vegas 42
5. Las Vegas with Kids 48
6. Thrill-seekers' Las Vegas 52
7. Romantic Las Vegas 56
8. Old West Las Vegas 60
9. Gamblers' Las Vegas 65
10. Budget Las Vegas 72
11. Lake Mead and the Valley of Fire 76
12. Hoover Dam and Grand Canyon West 79

ART ENTHUSIASTS

Route 3 focuses on the city's main fine arts attractions, such as the 18B Arts District and Wynn Las Vegas. Out in the Valley of Fire (route 11) are stunning, ancient petroglyphs.

RECOMMENDED ROUTES FOR...

CHILDREN

Attractions such as Circus Circus and the city's many magic shows (route 5), as well as Shark Reef and the Lion Habitat Ranch (route 2), are sure to keep the kids happy. Even a ride on the monorail (route 6) guarantees lots of fun.

DAREDEVILS

Route 6 is designed for adrenaline junkies; with activities from Dig This to skydiving. You might also try the Skywalk at Grand Canyon West (route 12).

GAMBLERS

It's hard to come to Vegas and not get bitten by the gambling bug. Route 9 gives the lowdown on the best games, but you can also check out the Lost Vegas Gambling Museum and Shop (route 1), and the cheap-and-cheerful Slots-A-Fun (route 10).

HISTORY HUNTERS

Beneath the glitz are reminders of an interesting past. Pioneer-era destinations include the Nevada State Museum (route 8), while the Flamingo (route 1) is where "Bugsy" Siegel started it all.

MUSEUM BUFFS

It may be a surprise to find that Las Vegas has a wide range of museums, including the Marjorie Barrick Museum and Arboretum (route 2), the Neon Museum (route 3) and the Lost City Museum (route 11).

NATURE LOVERS

Get back to nature at the Las Vegas Natural History Museum (route 8), gaze upon white tigers, lions, sharks, and dolphins (route 2), or explore the Botanical Gardens that are part of what's on offer at Ethel M's Chocolate Factory (route 7).

OUTDOOR TYPES

Go horseback riding at Red Rock Canyon (route 8) or pick one of the hiking trails in the Valley of Fire or off the Northshore Road (route 11), or around Lake Las Vegas (route 7).

CAESARS
PALACE
SINATRA

Wedding Chapel

INTRODUCTION

An introduction to Las Vegas's geography, customs and culture, plus illuminating background information on cuisine, history and what to do when you're there.

Explore Las Vegas	10
Food and Drink	16
Shopping	18
Gambling	20
Weddings	22
History: Key Dates	24

EXPLORE LAS VEGAS

If you haven't visited Las Vegas lately, you're in for a revelation. Formerly a notorious den of iniquity, where gambling reigned supreme, "Sin City" has been transformed over the last decade or so into a giant, multibillion-dollar adult amusement park.

Las Vegas attracts over 38 million visitors a year, making it one of the most popular tourist destinations on earth. It started with gambling and made a name for itself in the shotgun wedding business, but neither of those is the main draw for visitors today. Warm winters, excellent dining and shopping, the world's largest resort hotels, fine arts, great golf, and championship sporting events – and of course, the biggest names in stage entertainment – make for an exciting mix that even non-gamblers can't resist.

THE STRIP

When most people think of Las Vegas, the part they usually have in mind is the four-mile (6km) stretch of Las Vegas Boulevard South known as the Strip, which is lined with America's biggest and most famous casino resorts. Oddly enough, the Strip is not officially part of Las Vegas. Ever since development began there in the 1930s, property owners along the Strip, keen to avoid local taxation and regulation (and originally to stay outside of local police jurisdiction), have successfully blocked all attempts to annex it into municipal Las Vegas or establish it as a separate town and it remains an unincorporated area of Clark County.

The center of the action along the Strip has moved over the years. Resort development originally started around the intersection with Flamingo Road and moved north past Desert Inn Road to Sahara Avenue. When the

The Wynn

The Strip

themed mega-resort boom came in the 1990s, construction moved south, spanning from Flamingo Road to Tropicana Avenue and into the underdeveloped land past Tropicana. Now this area has been built up to near capacity, and many of the older hotels along the length of the Strip have been razed to make way for new, even more ambitious projects.

Today, from the Fashion Show Mall south, most property has been consolidated into a few enormously ambitious multiple-use projects, combining resort hotels, condominium complexes, and retail space. These include Echelon Place, Project CityCenter, and the twin-towered Trump International, costing billions of dollars each.

OFF-STRIP

Large resort hotels have also been built within a mile or two east and west of the Strip. The trend started in 1969 with the building of the International Hotel near the original Las Vegas Convention Center, east of the north end of the Strip. The International would become famed as the concert venue of such top Vegas headliners as Elvis Presley, Liberace, and Barbra Streisand. Later, as the convention center expanded to become one of the largest in America, the International was replaced by the Las Vegas Hilton, the largest of several business-class hotels along Paradise Road and Convention Center Drive.

More recent off-Strip resort development has focused on two areas near the southern Strip. Across Interstate 25, West Flamingo Road is the site of several major high-rise resorts including the Rio Suites and the Palms, site of a number of top nightclubs and concert venues. To the east, along Paradise Road between the Strip and the University of Nevada (Las Vegas campus), major resorts include the hip Hard Rock Hotel, and the well-appointed non-gaming Alexis Park Resort.

Las Vegas is the fastest-growing city in the US, so new residential areas

Water attraction

In an arid desert, Las Vegas's fast growth and the importance to tourism of water attractions such as huge, elaborate pools, and the Bellagio's fountains have created a water crisis. The Vegas Springs Preserve (333 South Valley View Boulevard; tel: 702-822-7736; www.lvspringspreserve.org; daily 10am–10pm) is a multimillion-dollar effort to educate the public about water conservation with interactive exhibits, demonstration gardens and even a simulated flash flood. It also features a re-creation of the original springs that brought explorers and ranchers to the valley, as well as an arboretum of plants from the various North American deserts and 2 miles (3km) of hiking trails through the natural Mojave landscape. Great for kids!

The entrance to Caesars Palace

DON'T LEAVE VEGAS WITHOUT...

Watching the fountains in front of the Bellagio. The performances take place in front of the hotel and are completely free to watch. Probably the best time to watch a display is at night, when the colors of the lights and the spraying water itself is more prominent against the dark night sky. See page 45.

Seeing the "canals" at the Venetian Hotel. Inside the hotel complex is a 500,000-sq-foot (46,500-sq-meter) upscale shopping mall called the Grand Canal Shoppes, styled to look exactly like the tranquil aquatic arteries of that famous semi-sunken Italian city. See page 44.

Marveling at the Hoover Dam. A short journey from Las Vegas is this awe-inspiring tribute to American engineering. Construction began back in 1931 and was completed in 1936. Whilst bidding to be host city for this flagship project, the city was forced to clean up its seedy image, and the Las Vegas we know today was born. See page 79.

Visiting Fremont Street. The second most famous street in the Las Vegas Valley after the Strip dates back to 1905, when Las Vegas itself was founded. It's where many famous casinos, such as the Eldorado Club, the Fremont Hotel and the Golden Nugget, are located. See page 28.

Visiting the Las Vegas Springs. The whole reason Vegas is where it is, is right here. Once you've taken in the glitz and the glamour of the Strip, take a trip out to the Las Vegas Springs Preserve, which is built around the original water source for the city. See page 77.

Getting hands-on at Grand Canyon West. Further east from the Hoover Dam is Grand Canyon West, an activity venter where there are several experiences on offer: walk along a glass-floored walkway, 4,000ft (1,219 meters) above the Grand Canyon floor; see the Grand Canyon by helicopter tour; or go white-water rafting down the Colorado River. See page 80.

Indulging your sweet tooth at Ethel M's Chocolate Factory and Botanical Gardens. Take a guided tour and learn how Ethel M make their famous range of chocolate goods and see the botanical gardens, which feature over 300 different species of desert plants. There is also a small M&M World, so after you've worked up an appetite, sample some of the goods for yourself! See page 58.

Visiting the Neon Museum. Many of the old iconic neon signs were destined for scrap, but thankfully, that didn't happen, and the Neon Museum, located on Las Vegas Boulevard and Bonanza Road, now has many of these pieces in its collection. See page 37.

Having a beer at the Yard House. Located near the Linq, the food here is excellent and there's a choice of literally hundreds of different craft beers, bitters, and ales on draft. See page 96.

The Luxor

The Palms' Ditch Fridays Pool Party

spring up seemingly overnight. Since completion of the freeway linking it with McCarren International Airport and the Strip area, the once one-horse, magnesium-mining town of Henderson, southeast of Las Vegas, has boomed into a sprawling bedroom community of more than 250,000 people, displacing Reno as Nevada's second-largest city. Henderson also has numerous casino resorts, from budget options such as the Fiesta to the luxurious Green Valley Ranch Resort and Spa.

DOWNTOWN

Formerly nicknamed "Glitter Gulch" until city fathers tried to shed its dubious reputation by renaming it "the Fremont Street Experience," Fremont Street is the center of the action in Downtown Las Vegas and many serious gamblers prefer the Downtown casinos for their lack of touristic distractions. The five-block pedestrian-only section of Fremont has 10 casino hotels, a single, somewhat sleazy but historic striptease joint, and the world's largest LED screen, four blocks long and 90ft (27 meters) above the street, where the spectacular, free Viva Vision extravaganzas are shown nightly. To the west, a run-down area on the edge of Downtown has been redeveloped as the 18b Arts District, a studio and gallery zone that comes to life with big street celebrations, once a month (see page 38).

Casino at the Encore

AROUND THE CITY

As you will see if you fly into Las Vegas during daylight hours, the metropolitan area is surrounded by a vast, unpopulated desert, the Mojave. To the east, and hidden from the city by a jagged, barren mountain range, lies Lake Mead, created during the 1930s by damming the confluence of the Colorado and Virgin rivers. Near the Henderson entrance to Lake Mead National Recreation Area, the much smaller, similarly man-made Lake Las Vegas has condominiums, a golf course, and several luxury resort hotels.

To the southwest stand the Spring Mountains, with the stately 11,916-ft (3,632-meter) Mt. Charleston as their

Drai's Beachclub and Nightclub

centerpiece. Here, Las Vegas visitors are often amazed to find evergreen forests and alpine wilderness covered with snow more than half the year. The mountainside has a ski area, and a small, rustic year-round hotel, the Mt. Charleston Inn.

CLIMATE

Due to its desert location, Las Vegas has an extremely dry climate. The average annual rainfall is a scant, unpredictable 4 inches (10cm), with no more than half an inch (1cm) falling in any single month. Summer temperatures are hot, with typical daytime highs of 100–106°F (38–41°C). However, as most activities take place in air-conditioned comfort, Las Vegas is a year-round tourist destination with no noticeable low-season slump. Winter low temperatures hardly ever dip below freezing, with daytime highs usually in the upper 50s°F and 60s°F (16–21°C). Because the humidity is too low to hold much heat, at all times of year the temperature drops by about 30°F (17°C) when the sun goes down.

Skywalk at Grand Canyon West

PEOPLE

Fifty percent of Las Vegas residents are of European ancestry, 28.6 percent are of Latin American ancestry, and 11.3 percent are black. The Chinese, although accounting for a mere 4.8 percent of the population, are the city's fastest-growing minority group. Only 0.7 percent of Las Vegas residents are American Indians. About 19 percent of the people who live in Las Vegas are legal immigrants to the States, though only one-third of them have become naturalized US citizens.

As of 2015, the US Census Bureau reports that the median household income for the greater Las Vegas area was $50,903, which is about 7 percent above the national average. But the per capita income was only $26,752, which is significantly below the national

WELCOME TO *Fabulous* LAS VEGAS NEVADA

average. This apparent contradiction is explained by Las Vegas's young population, with an extraordinarily large percentage of children and teens who are not part of the workforce and a large percentage of two-income families.

TOP TIPS FOR VISITING LAS VEGAS

Sun and heat. Sunburn and even sunstroke are a risk in Las Vegas – it's in a valley after all. During the summer temperatures can soar, so it's important to stay hydrated.

Cash. Most ATMs located in casinos will charge quite a lot to withdraw from, so try to take money out from banks and cash machines away from the Strip. Take more out and use them less.

Touts. Avoid any ticket touts offering seemingly amazing deals on the streets. Chances are they're fake, or at least overpriced. Always buys tickets to events through official channels.

Get your money's worth. If you dine at a quality, expensive restaurant, and there are plenty to choose from, don't be afraid to ask for what you want, even if it's not on the menu.

Check prices. There are too many traps to count in Las Vegas, all designed specifically to separate you from your hard-earned cash. If the price isn't shown, don't be afraid to ask.

Hangovers. The air can be quite dry in Vegas – add that to a night of hard drinking and what you get in the morning is the hangover from hell. Stay hydrated and buy water from a local 7-Eleven to keep in your room.

Mini-bars. For the love of God, don't disturb anything in the mini-bar. Think of them as minefields. Even if you don't actually use anything, it all sits on extremely sensitive sensors; even if it's just moved, it registers and you'll get charged for it.

Walking distances. Be aware that the distances between hotels and casinos are a lot further than they may appear on the map or smartphone app. Add the amount of walking once you're inside the casinos and that equals a lot of time on your feet.

Take lessons. A lot of the hotels and casinos offer lessons in gambling – don't be afraid to sign up for a few, it might make the visit more fun. Always remember to gamble responsibly.

Big stakes. Be aware of what the minimum stakes are at the table. In casinos on the Strip, like Caesars and the Bellagio, chances are they are a *lot* higher than they might be on Fremont Street.

Off Strip. Remember, there are a lot of good places to go that are off the Strip; Vegas is a lot more than just the Strip. Explore Fremont Street and even go Downtown.

Locals. If you do head Downtown, remember this is home to the hundreds of thousands of people that work in Vegas. Be respectful. Don't be a drunken idiot here, or anywhere else for that matter.

Traffic. Regardless of which country you come from, or what country you're visiting, force yourself to get into the habit of looking both ways every single time you cross a road.

Breakfast at Serendipity 3, Caesars Palace

FOOD AND DRINK

In an earlier era, Las Vegas was known for 99-cent breakfasts and ridiculously cheap all-you-can-eat buffets, but times have changed. These can still be found, but these days on the Strip, you're seldom more than a few minutes' walk from a $200 dinner.

Way back in 1992, Wolfgang Puck opened his first Vegas location, Spago, in Caesars Palace, which proved that upscale restaurants could draw capacity crowds in casino resorts. As a result, food quality drastically improved and this trend is still evident today; hotel coffee shops serve gourmet breakfasts and casino buffets have been transformed into smorgasbords of international cuisine. There is even a fast-food restaurant that offers $60 Kobe beef burgers.

WHERE TO EAT

Every large resort has restaurants – some as many as 15 of them – in every price, ranging from no-frills coffee shops to luxe eateries. You might expect the patrons at the celebrity-chef signature restaurants found in every major resort to be high rollers on winning streaks, but most serious gamblers prefer buffets. Big-name, big-price restaurants thrive because of lovers' trysts, wedding receptions, family reunions, and all the many occasions for making a vacation as unforgettable as possible, regardless of the expense.

Global choice

Since Las Vegas has no regional cuisine of its own, most of its restaurants feature international menus representing one country or another. For instance, Paris Las Vegas has French restaurants including an elegant dining room midway up the Eiffel Tower and an upscale room filled with the paintings of Pablo Picasso. Other hotels offer great Italian, Japanese, and Mexican restaurants – as well as the ubiquitous steakhouse and seafood-serving outlets.

Themed restaurants and shows

Restaurants focused around a particular theme have proliferated in Vegas. Local versions of the Hard Rock Café and the Harley-Davidson Café pull in brisk business and then there are international

Food and Drink prices

Price guide for an average two-course meal for one with a glass of house wine:

$$$$ = over $60
$$$ = $40–60
$$ = $20–40
$ = under $20

estaurant in New York New York

Cocktails at Carnival World Buffet

themed eateries, from the imposing Hofbrauhaus to a rainforest eatery complete with thunderstorms.

Bountiful buffets

Casinos still have buffets, but many of them have been transformed from the cheap-eats cafeterias of old into lavish spreads featuring foods from around the world as well as the usual prime rib, shrimp, and crab. Despite the improvement of the city's culinary landscape as a whole, buffets can still be a hit-and-miss affair, but the Rio's Carnival World Buffet is a cut above. No longer as affordable as they once were, most all-you-can-eat buffets cost $30 to $40, though some in older hotels still charge less than $20.

EATING HOURS

Las Vegas may be open all night, but most of its restaurants are not. Many upscale and mid-range outlets only serve dinner until 10 or 11pm during the week and an hour later at weekends. However, virtually all casinos have some kind of coffee shop that serves snacks 24 hours a day. If you plan to dine at any resort restaurants other than buffets or coffee shops, make reservations as soon as possible.

BEVERAGES

Alcohol fits right into the Sin City image, and it's common to see people staggering along the Strip in various states of inebriation, day or night. In fact, if you're gambling in a casino – even slowly for low stakes – waitresses will keep bringing you complimentary drinks. The reason is simple: casino managers know that the more you drink, the more money you will lose. Ultimately, it costs less to gamble sober and pay for your drinks.

Penalties for excess

Things change outside the casino. Drunken pedestrians are tolerated, but Las Vegas is one of the highest-risk cities in the US for alcohol-related traffic accidents, so the local police take driving under the influence very seriously. There are "sobriety checkpoints" all over town. Drivers who test over 0.8 percent blood-alcohol content are likely to spend the night in jail, post bond the next day, and return to Vegas months later to stand trial. First-time drink driving (DUI) offenses are punished by mandatory jail sentences.

Dining on a budget

Eating on a tight budget in Vegas isn't as easy as it used to be, but it's still possible. Look for buffets and coffee shops in the older hotels on the Strip, such as the Flamingo and Tropicana, or head towards Downtown. Check out unique budget dining options listed in this book, such as Vickie's Diner in White Cross Drug (www.vickiesdiner.com) and Little Tony's on West Sahara Avenue (www.littletonyslasvegas.com).

Forum Shops, Caesars Palace

SHOPPING

Although locals complain that "real world" shopping in Las Vegas is somewhat mundane, there is no question that the Strip has become one of America's top upscale shopping areas, rivaling Beverly Hills' Rodeo Drive and Palm Beach's Worth Avenue.

Not so long ago, shopping possibilities in Las Vegas were so dismal that many locals drove 300 miles (480km) to Los Angeles for whatever they couldn't buy at their neighborhood convenience store. The ruling powers believed that spending in stores competed with losing money in the casinos. But then a few resorts, such as the original MGM Grand, opened small, expensive shopping areas where players who got lucky in the casinos could spend their winnings – or spouses could spend while their partners gambled. Back in the 1990s, exclusive boutiques, shops, and designer outlets proliferated; today many visitors bypass gambling altogether, preferring to spend their time in the labyrinth of high-end malls.

STRIP SHOPPING

Most large casino resorts now have shopping zones. Some, such as the stores in Circus Circus and the Excalibur, are oriented toward families and children. Others are essentially department store-size versions of standard hotel gift shops, specializing in swimwear and items bearing the hotel logo.

Retail fantasies

The best of the resort shopping malls are truly spectacular. Don't miss the atmospheric malls at theme hotels, such as Paris Las Vegas's Le Boulevard, the Venetian's Grand Canal Shoppes, or the Via Bellagio, at the hotel of the same name. The Wynn Esplanade is so exclusive that its retailers include a Ferrari-Maserati dealership. The Miracle Mile Shops at the Planet Hollywood (formerly the Aladdin) has no fewer than 170 sleek, trendy stores, but the long-established Forum Shops in Caesars Palace still reigns supreme in the realm of ultra-expensive designer boutiques.

Fashion Show Mall

With its center-Strip location, the huge, upscale Fashion Show Mall was expanded in 2003 to nearly three times its original size – it now has more than 200 stores and restaurants – making it one of the largest shopping malls in the US. It is also the only one that has six of the country's highest-quality department store chains – Bloomingdales, Macy's, Dillard's, Nordstrom, Neiman Marcus, and Saks Fifth Avenue – under the same roof.

Gamblers General Store

Glass shop in the Venetian

BEYOND THE STRIP

Most visitors find it unnecessary to leave the Strip to indulge their wildest shopping fantasies. Off-Strip possibilities are rather limited. For instance, the much-anticipated Downtown mall Neonopolis has developed into an entertainment complex of restaurants, nightclubs, a huge video arcade, and a 14-screen movie theater, fringed with novelty shops.

MALLS OFF THE STRIP

Of the several malls that have sprung up to serve the burgeoning eastern suburbs, The Boulevard, located about five miles (8km) from the Strip at 3528 South Maryland Parkway, is the largest. While it has about the same number of retail stores as the Fashion Show Mall, The Boulevard covers a larger area – 1.2 million sq ft (111,484 sq meters) – and so claims the distinction of being Nevada's largest mall. Many of the stores here are the same ones as you'll find in every major shopping mall in America.

A unique Las Vegas shopping experience, Chinatown Plaza at 4255 Spring Mountain Road is the largest collection of Asian retail stores and restaurants in the state. The mall was created to accommodate Hong Kong businesspeople seeking to relocate to the US during the 1990s, when Hong Kong came under Chinese rule. Its success has come largely from the growing numbers of Chinese and other Asian visitors who come to Las Vegas each year. Besides an Asian supermarket and numerous gift shops, you will find a Chinese bookstore, a medicinal herb shop, and a jewelry store that specializes in jade.

Las Vegas Chinatown

Outlet opportunities

Downtown also has a relatively new outlet store complex, Las Vegas Premium Outlets, with shops such as Ann Taylor, Eddie Bauer, Guess, Armani Exchange, Bose, and Polo Ralph Lauren offering savings of 25 to 65 percent off regular list prices.

Many outlet store buffs also make excursions across the desert to Fashion Outlets of Las Vegas, located 40 miles (64km) south on I-15 (Exit 1) in the town of Primm. While many of the 100 stores here are the same as those in Las Vegas Premium Outlets, the atmosphere is more relaxing, it's a lot less crowded and the remote location makes it a fun trip.

Craps class at the MGM Grand

GAMBLING

There is just one guaranteed way to make money from a casino: buy one. If you gamble in Las Vegas, do it for fun and see any profit as a bonus. Set a limit before, do not exceed it and quit while you're ahead. For our gambling route, see page 65.

You may have Lady Luck on your side when you play, but then again you may not. Serious players pre-calculate a stake range – highest to lowest bet – by multiplying the number of hours they intend to play by the number of games per hour, and dividing their "bankroll" by the result, to set a maximum stake. A low stake is then set at around 20 percent of the maximum, or less. Low bets are made until a winning streak is hit, then stakes are progressively raised.

It's a good idea to ride a winning streak. If you strike it lucky, put a profit to one side, then raise your stakes and go for it. If you start to lose, cut back or – better still – walk away. Playing comfortably low stakes offers more fun in the long run. Betting $5 one hundred times and winning some of the time gives more hours of entertainment than playing $500 and maybe losing, once.

BLACKJACK

Blackjack offers some of the best odds in the casino. The house's natural edge is between 3 and 5 percent, and skilled players can narrow that to 0.5 percent with betting and playing combinations.

The object is to get a hand of cards closer to 21 than the dealer. Cards take their numerical value, except for face cards counting as 10, and aces, which the player can value as one or 11. The top hand, an ace with a 10 or a picture, makes 21 or "blackjack."

Blackjack deals are usually from a six- or eight-deck plastic "shoe." Some – mostly downtown – casinos play with a single deck, giving the player much better chances to predict the remaining cards, but payouts are usually lower.

CRAPS

A craps game may look daunting, but it's really quite simple. It also offers good odds to players. Bets are made for and against a dice roll, called "right" or "wrong" bets. The dice pass around the table. No-one has to roll, but the thrower must bet on his own game.

At the first, or "come out" roll, a throw of 2, 3, or 12 is known as craps. This is a win for bets on the "don't pass" line, or wrong bets. The numbers 7 or 11 are automatic winners for "pass-line" right bets. Any other number rolled establishes the shooter's "point." The aim

Blackjack tables

Mirage Sports Book

then is to roll the point again before hitting a 7.

KENO

Keno is hugely popular because it is so simple to play, and a $50,000 payout is possible on a $1 bet. All you need do is pick some numbers on a ticket and wait. It's easy, and it's fun. It's also among the lowest player odds in the house, with a casino edge of 20 to 30 percent.

Due to a mystery of Nevada gaming regulation, Keno is not, technically, a lottery. Pay-outs must be collected immediately after each game, and before the next game starts, or they are forfeited. Take a place at the bar or café and call a Keno runner over, pick your lucky numbers and wait for the draw. If the runner returns with winnings, it's polite to tip.

ROULETTE

The wheel spins, the ball spins against it. The ball drops, and clatters. It bounces once, twice, and comes to rest in number 7. The dealer places the white marker next to your chip on the 7, and your $100 bet is joined by $3,500 in chips.

Or not. Pay out can be a dizzying 35 to 1, but the 0 and 00 make the odds of you predicting the right number 37 to 1. If the ball falls on 0 or 00, all bets lose, except those predicting that exact outcome. This makes the overall house edge 5.6 percent, and about the poorest table odds in town. The safest bets on the wheel are the outsiders; the "dozens" (first 12, second 12, or third 12), which pays out 2 to 1. Otherwise, 1 to 1 payouts are offered by "red or black," "odd or even," or "first or last 18."

SPORTS BOOKS

In the Sports Book, players rely on their expertise in predicting sports events, such as football, baseball, Indy car races, and championship boxing. But the main event in the book is horse racing, still the largest spectator sport in the US. A horse's previous performance, or "form," is a guide, and the simple bets – "win" or "place" – are the most profitable.

POKER

The ability to read other players at the table can be as important in poker as getting the best cards. Players who think they have the strongest hand will try to lure money into the "pot," but players who believe they have weaker cards may bluff, to scare others out of the game. Poker is the only game where play is against other gamblers and not against the house. Instead, the house gets a cut off the top of each pot.

A common form of poker in Vegas is Texas Hold 'em. Each player is dealt two cards, face down. Through progressive betting rounds, five "community cards" are dealt, face up. Each player then makes the highest five-card hand they can from the seven cards available.

Cupid's Wedding Chapel

WEDDINGS

Las Vegas is a favorite destination not only for gambling and conventions, but also as a mecca of matrimony, a paradise of promises, a Valhalla for vows. Over 174,000 troths are pledged here every single year.

Vegas originally became a wedding capital because only in Nevada could you get a marriage license without a blood test and a waiting period. Today, only a handful of states require either one so the only real advantage to getting married in Las Vegas is that you can get a wedding license in the middle of the night.

STATISTICS

Vegas has around 50 wedding chapels, which open daily from 8am to midnight (24 hours on legal holidays), from the gimmicky drive-thru to slightly more dignified wedding chapels. There are also elegant wedding gardens and most major resorts on the Strip have their own wedding chapels too.

The invitation to impulsiveness is taken advantage of by an average of 337 couples every day, though over Valentine's Day weekend as many as 2,000 are married. At least 87,000 marriage licenses, each costing $55, are issued each year.

CELEBRITY WEDDINGS

Celebrity weddings have been fashionable in Sin City since silent-film stars Clara Bow and Rex Bell chose to tie the knot here.

The golden years

Perhaps the first marriage that grabbed the public's attention took place in 1943, when Betty Grable and trumpeter and band leader Harry James exchanged their vows at the Little Church of the West. The *Las Vegas Review-Journal* reported that more than 100 locals left their beds in the middle of the night to make a trip to the train station, hoping to get a glimpse of Grable as she waited for James to return from Mexico with his divorce papers. The wedding took place just before dawn, and after the ceremony, the couple drove back to Los Angeles.

Mickey Rooney married Ava Gardner at the same spot in January 1942. Over the next three decades he made seven return trips to the same chapel, concluding with a marriage to January Chamberlin in 1978.

Among other famous marriages at that busy chapel was that of Zsa Zsa Gabor and actor George Sanders in 1949. In the same year, Rita Hayworth married singer Dick Haymes at the Sands and on

Stratosphere Wedding Chapel

Newlyweds on top of the Stratosphere

July 19, 1966 Ol' Blue Eyes married Mia Farrow at the Sands, Sinatra's second home for nearly a decade.

Ongoing trend

The trend for quickie Vegas-style nuptials looks set to continue. Billy Bob Thornton married Angelina Jolie in 2000 at the Little Church of the West and in January 2004, Britney Spears married Jason Allen Alexander at the Little White Chapel, although the marriage was famously annulled 55 hours later. In 2011 Sinéad O'Connor married Barry Herridge, also at the Little White Chapel.

THEMED NUPTIALS

However, it's the more colorful ceremonies for which Las Vegas is most well-known. Viva Las Vegas Wedding Chapel at the northern end of the Strip offers a Blue Hawaiian wedding named after the Elvis movie, as well as a pink Cadillac wedding, a Star Trek-themed wedding, and a Woodstock wedding.

The Excalibur provides a medieval-inspired ceremony and the MGM Grand offers Merlin the wizard to officiate while a fire-breathing dragon attempts to thwart the nuptials. Betrothals can be made by, with, or even to the Phantom of the Opera. Other options include a beach party, a Wild West wedding on horseback, a pirate ship, the Las Vegas Motor Speedway, the bottom of the Grand Canyon, under water and the top of Paris Las Vegas's Eiffel Tower.

EXTREME WEDDINGS

Those with a taste for the extreme can marry on a bungee jump, during a roller-coaster ride or, for even whiter knuckles, during a parachute jump or sky-dive. Ceremonies can be officiated in a helicopter hovering over the Strip, the Grand Canyon, or the Hoover Dam. For more serene mid-air marriages, a hot-air balloon is available with a basket large enough for bride, groom, and the assembled company.

ON FOUR WHEELS

One wedding chapel offers a drive-thru venue, so the bride and groom don't even need to leave their car. For the more upmarket autophile, you can have a limousine drive to the scenic backdrop of your choice – and get married in the back of the stretch. In fact, a few limos come equipped with whirlpools and hot tubs, so the happy couple can bubble and betroth simultaneously.

Wedding outfits

Catering to Vegas's wedding market are numerous bride stores. These include I&A Formalwear (4850 West Flamingo Road; tel: 702-364-5777) and Bridal de Paris (2207 Las Vegas Boulevard South; tel: 702-301-1002), where packages include hair, makeup, and clothes for the bride, bridesmaids, and mother of the bride.

Roulette at a Casino, circa 1930

HISTORY: KEY DATES

Barely 105 years old, Las Vegas has always had a pioneering spirit. A magnet for stars and celebrities, it has one of the most colorful histories of all US cities, one that is played out against a backdrop of constant transformation.

EARLY HISTORY

11,000 BC.	Paleo-Indians first hunt big game in the cool, lush Las Vegas Valley.
AD 1150	Paiute Indians begin to winter in the Las Vegas Valley.
1829	Mexican trader Antonio Armijo camps near desert springs and names the area Las Vegas, Spanish for "the meadows".
1844	Noted explorer John C. Fremont, leading an overland expedition, camps at a site that as a tribute to him years later becomes known as Fremont Street, in downtown Las Vegas.

PIONEER YEARS

1848	US acquires the region by treaty after winning the Mexican War.
1855–7	Mormons found a settlement in Las Vegas to convert the Paiutes.
1902	San Pedro, Los Angeles, and Salt Lake City Railroad (later known as Union Pacific) buys land and lays out Las Vegas.
1908	Telephone and water lines are established in the region.
1911	The city of Las Vegas is incorporated on March 16.

GOLDEN AGE

1920	The first Vegas gaming hall, the Northern Club, is opened in Downtown's Fremont Street.
1931	Gambling in Nevada is legalized.
1935	President Franklin D. Roosevelt dedicates Hoover Dam.
1946	Mobster Benjamin "Bugsy" Siegel opens the Flamingo Hotel, attracting Hollywood stars to Las Vegas.
1955	Las Vegas's first high-rise hotel, the nine-story Riviera, is built.
1960	The Rat Pack comes to town.

Fremont Street in 1967

MODERN LAS VEGAS

1989	The Mirage casino opens with 3,039 rooms.
1990	Las Vegas's population reaches 258,295, doubling in just a decade.
1992	The success of Warren Beatty's movie *Bugsy* prompts the Flamingo Hilton to open the Bugsy Celebrity Theater.
1993	The MGM Grand opens as the world's biggest resort.
1995	The Fremont Street Experience opens. Gaming revenues are $5.7 billion, 78 percent of the US total.
1997	New York-New York, a scaled-down version of Manhattan, opens.
1998	The Bellagio, the world's most expensive hotel ($1.7 billion), opens.

21ST CENTURY

2000	The Venetian opens. Vegas now has 19 of the world's 20 biggest hotels.
2002	Nevada is named the fastest-growing state in the US.
2003	Roy (of Siegfried & Roy) is badly mauled by one of the pair's tigers and the act is forced to close.
2004	The Harrah's group buys historic casino Binion's Horseshoe from the Binion family. In July, the long-awaited monorail opens.
2005	Steve Wynn's eponymous Wynn Las Vegas opens.
2007	The $1.9 billion Palazzo resort opens; the hotel complex is named the largest hotel in the world by the Guinness Book of World Records.
2008	OJ Simpson is found guilty of armed robbery and the kidnapping of two sports memorabilia dealers in Las Vegas, and sentenced to 33 years in prison.
2009	The CityCenter complex opens and is the largest privately funded construction project in the history of the United States.
2010	The enormous Cosmopolitan luxury resort casino and hotel opens, with 2,995 rooms.
2012	The UK's Prince Harry is photographed naked whilst partying in a Las Vegas hotel.
2013	Britney Spears kicks off her Las Vegas casino residency.
2014	The High Roller, a 500-ft (152-meter) observation wheel, opens.
2015	Fire engulfs the 14th floor of the Cosmopolitan hotel, causing $2m worth of damage.

BEST ROUTES

1. Classic Las Vegas	28
2. All-natural Vegas	32
3. Artistic Las Vegas	36
4. International Vegas	42
5. Las Vegas with Kids	48
6. Thrill-seekers' Las Vegas	52
7. Romantic Las Vegas	56
8. Old West Las Vegas	60
9. Gamblers' Las Vegas	65
10. Budget Las Vegas	72
11. Lake Mead and the Valley of Fire	76
12. Hoover Dam and Grand Canyon West	79

CLASSIC LAS VEGAS

From the late 1940s to the mid-1970s, the city's mix of high life and low life made it unique in the annals of American pop culture. While visitors today find little to remind them of that era, nostalgia buffs who search for it can still discover traces of old-time Vegas.

DISTANCE: 10 miles (16km)
TIME: 10 hours (including dinner and a show)
START: Fremont Street
END: Greek Isles Hotel
POINTS TO NOTE: This route can be done by car, taxi, or CAT bus (routes 108 and 117). If you choose to continue the tour into the evening, order tickets for the show well in advance, especially if going on a Saturday. Please note, there are no performances on Fridays.

One of America's youngest cities, Las Vegas nonetheless has quite a past, and this route provides the ideal way to discover it. The route takes you from the area known as Downtown, where it all started, to what could arguably be described as *the* classic Vegas hotel, and on to an evening show that will transport you back to the good old days of the Rat Pack.

If you haven't already had breakfast, and are coming from the Strip, we recommend you set yourself up for the day with breakfast at **Tiffany's Café**, see 1.

DOWNTOWN

Fremont Street

At the northern end of the Strip is Downtown, where gambling started in Las Vegas. Its main thoroughfare is **Fremont Street** 1. If it's not too hot – which it may be in summer despite the shade afforded by the vaulted projection screen 90ft (27 meters) above street level – stroll up the five-block pedestrians-only section of the street.

Despite attempts to make it super-respectable, Downtown still has more old-time flavor than the Strip: look out for classic neon signs such as Vegas Vic and Vegas Vickie; spin a slot machine at Binion's Gambling Hall, founded in 1947 by legendary Texas bootlegger and convicted murderer Benny Binion, chief rival of the mobsters who built the Strip around the same time; and sip a cold drink at the Fremont, where Wayne "Mr. Vegas" Newton made his singing debut in 1959.

Fremont Street

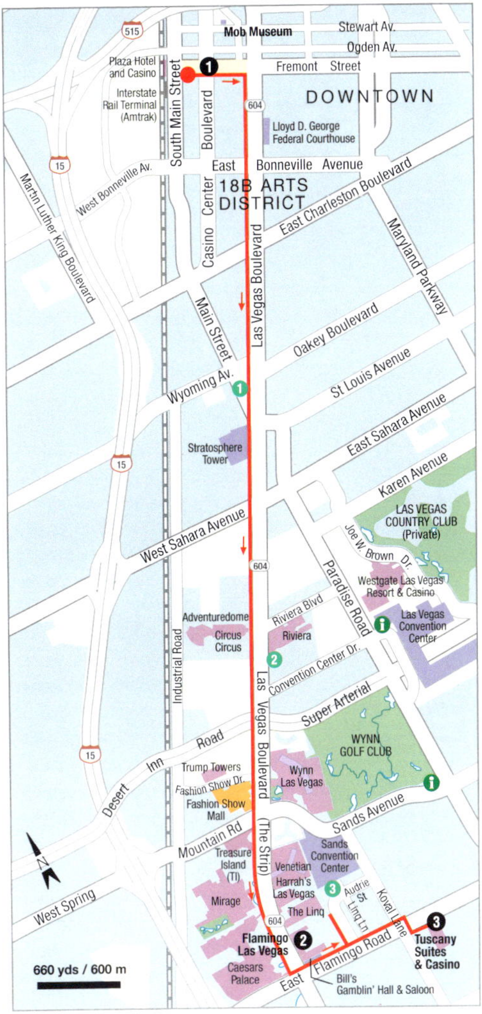

Here, too, is the now-posh Golden Nugget, where billionaire hotel developer Steve Wynn got his start in the days when Downtown was dusty, disreputable, and sleazy.

In the morning, the street is an easygoing place, where you can relax over coffee in a streetside café, then wander up to the renewed Fremont East Historic District around Neonopolis for a look at the outdoor Neon Museum's collection of old-time signs. After dark it becomes the Fremont Street Experience, featuring the world's largest light show (see page 75), and live entertainment on two stages, all free.

Neonopolis

Lined with over 3 miles of neon lights, it's pretty much impossible to miss **Neonopolis** (450 Fremont Street; 702-243-0654; www.neonopolislv.com), a 250,000-sq-ft (23,226-sq-meter) entertainment complex. Please note, there is a charge for parking.

Elvis impersonators on the Strip

Allow some time to enjoy this impressive shopping mall/entertainment complex. There are three levels in total: level one consists of retail outlets, restaurants, and even a tattoo parlour; level two is home to the **Southern Nevada Museum of Fine Art**; whilst several television studios occupy level three.

Elvis impersonators

Perhaps the biggest Las Vegas celebrity of all time (in more ways than one), Elvis Presley has inspired more tribute performers, or impersonators, than any other celebrity in history. In Vegas, impersonators have become such a cliché that professional Elvis tribute shows are fewer than they once were, though you'll still come across costumed Elvises on the street, and many wedding chapels offering ceremonies conducted by Elvis lookalikes. You can see a bronze statue of The King in the Las Vegas Hilton (3000 South Paradise Road; tel: 702-732-5111), which stands on the site of the old International Hotel where Elvis played 837 sell-out shows. Or, at Harrah's Las Vegas Hotel & Casino (3475 South Las Vegas Boulevard; tel: 800-214-9110), you may be able to catch a show by Big Elvis, the sometime 900-lb (408kg) entertainer, who has been known to take sabbaticals in order to lose weight. But the place wannabe Elvises most often congregate to see and be seen, in the hope of becoming the next star of the casino's long-running *Spirit of the King* lounge show, is the Four Queens Hotel and Casino (202 East Fremont Street; tel: 702-385-4011; www.fourqueens.com).

At this point in the tour it should be around lunchtime and a good time to take a break. As the tour continues by heading up the Strip, a good option en route is the **Peppermill Inn**, see ②.

THE FLAMINGO

Continue south on the Strip, all the way down to the **Flamingo** ❷ (3555 Las Vegas Boulevard South; tel: 702-733-3111/888-902-9929; www.flamingolv.com; see pages 34 and 88), the casino hotel that started it all.

Opened by mobster Benjamin "Bugsy" Siegel in 1946 as part of a money-laundering scheme, the hotel has been renovated beyond recognition by subsequent owners including Kirk Kerkorian and the Hilton Corporation, but you can still find a bronze plaque commemorating Siegel in the outdoor garden of the hotel's wedding chapel.

RAT PACK SHOW

If you want to continue the themed tour into the evening, our suggestion is an early dinner at **Battista's Hole in the Wall**, see ③, which is just behind the Flamingo, on Linq Lane, followed

The Rat Pack is Back

by a classic show, The Rat Pack is Back.

The show plays at the **Tuscany Suites & Casino** ❸ (255 East Flamingo Road; tel: 702-893-8933; www.tuscanylv.com; check website for show times), head away from the Strip on East Flamingo Road for a couple of blocks, and it's on your right.

This impersonator show reincarnates Frank Sinatra and his "Rat Pack" members, Dean Martin, Sammy Davis Jr., and Joey Bishop, who often performed together in the 1960s and became the era's most renowned Las Vegas celebrities. The gang are sent back from heaven (presumably) to "do it one more time" in Vegas. Conspicuously absent is fellow Rat Packer Peter Lawford. As J.F. Kennedy's brother-in-law, Lawford had no choice but to sever his ties with the Rat Pack, thus preventing Sinatra's alleged Mafia connections from embarrassing President Kennedy. The show ends at around 10.30pm.

Food and Drink

❶ TIFFANY'S CAFÉ

White Cross Drugstore, 1700 Las Vegas Boulevard South; tel: 702-444-4459; daily 24hr; $

Inexpensive breakfasts any time of the day or night used to be a Vegas hallmark. Today, one of the last places to find one is this old-time Greek-American lunch counter. It opened in the 1950s as the Liberty Café and is today an artists' hangout, located midway between Downtown and the central Strip.

❷ PEPPERMILL INN

2895 Las Vegas Boulevard South; tel: 702-735-7635; daily 24hr; $

Breakfast, lunch, dinner or late-night snack, you'll always find huge portions at this cozy restaurant and lounge toward the north end of the Strip. Entrées range from cheeseburgers and fries to Chilean sea bass. A restaurant since 1972, the Peppermill is rumored to have been a mobsters' meeting place in the old days. It is perhaps better known as the location for the 1995 movie *Casino*; Robert De Niro is said to have liked the restaurant so much that he continued to eat here after filming was done – and still does now when he's in town.

❸ BATTISTA'S HOLE IN THE WALL

4041 Linq Lane; tel: 702-732-1424; www.battistaslasvegas.com; daily 5–10.30pm; $$–$$$

Run by the same family for more than 30 years, this atmospheric Italian restaurant has walls covered with historic photos of its many celebrity patrons. All entrées come with soup or salad, house wine, garlic bread, and cappuccino. Reservations advised.

Siegfried and Roy's Secret Garden

ALL-NATURAL VEGAS

Las Vegas residents have a saying: "There's nature all over this town – human nature." Yet in fact, animal lovers will find a number of big-budget exhibits that most zoos would envy, as well as some beautiful indoor gardens.

DISTANCE: 24 miles (39km) (drive to Lion Habitat Ranch and back)
TIME: Roughly 9 hours
START/END: The Mirage
POINTS TO NOTE: All the sights on this tour except those at the university, the Lion Habitat Ranch and the Veggie House lunch recommendation are within walking distance. However, the CAT bus number 202 serves this route. This tour is a good one to do with children, if they are animal lovers.

It is, perhaps, ironic that a city such as Vegas that is so thoroughly artificial has so successfully managed to exploit some of nature's most dramatic protagonists, such as tigers, sharks, and lions. The fact that it has done so in its harsh and unforgiving desert location is truly impressive.

THE MIRAGE

Begin the tour at the **Mirage** ❶ (3400 Las Vegas Boulevard South; tel: 791-7111 or 800-929-1111; www.mirage.com; see pages 44 and 84), on the Strip. The inspiration for the array of widely emulated "theme" hotels on the Las Vegas Strip, the Mirage was the most expensive hotel ever built, costing $630 million in 1989.

It was the venue for Siegfried & Roy's animal magic show from 1990 to 2003, before the duo retired after Roy Horn was injured by a white tiger during their act. A larger-than-life statue of the duo and one of their tigers stands in front of the hotel. The Mirage has recently been remodeled to emphasize its exotic tropical nature theme, and looks over a model volcano. Guest rooms are luxurious, though somewhat small by modern Las Vegas standards.

You might like to start with an early (9am) breakfast at the hotel's casual **Paradise Café**, see ❶. After breakfast, take a look at the impressive, 53-ft (16-meter) -long, 20,000-gallon (75,700-liter) salt-water **aquarium** (daily; 24 hours; free) by the front desk that is home to 60 species of fish from the South Pacific Ocean, and the Caribbean Sea.

Dolphins at Mirage

Aquarium at Mirage

Siegfried and Roy's Secret Garden and Dolphin Habitat

At the end of the shopping promenade is this open-air jungle area (Mon–Fri 11am–5.30pm, Sat–Sun 10am–5.30pm; summer daily 10am–7pm) with waterfalls and a pool. The area is home to 40 rare or endangered species, including Siegfried & Roy's white tigers, and a white lion.

The white tigers, which live in conditions modeled on their natural habitat, are descendants of a breeding pair donated to a North American zoo by the Maharaja of Rewa, India, in 1958. They are not a distinct species, but the result of the appearance of a rare recessive gene. A larger pool with windows for underwater viewing is home to bottlenose dolphins, which are not trained to perform tricks but are provided with toys to play with on their own.

MARJORIE BARRICK MUSEUM AND ARBORETUM

At around noon, take a taxi or drive to the **Marjorie Barrick Museum and UNLV Arboretum** ❷ (4505 South Maryland Parkway; tel: 702-895-1421;

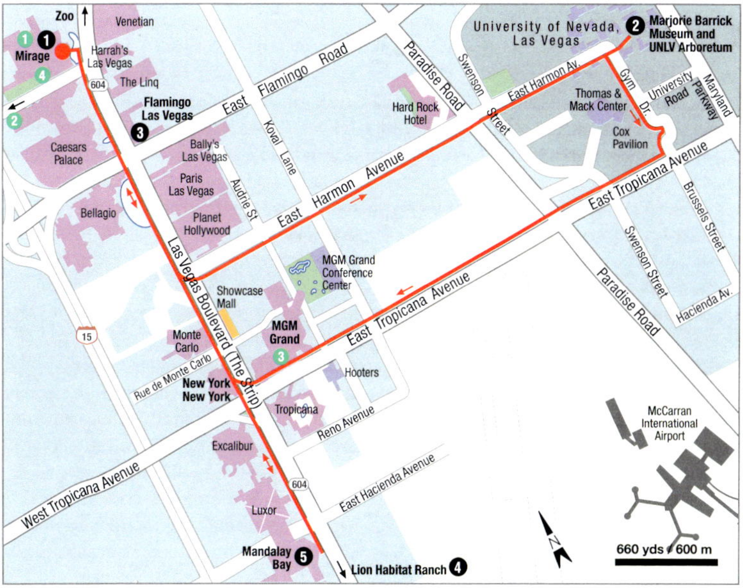

http://hrcweb.nevada.edu/Museum; Mon–Fri 9am–5pm, Sat noon–5pm, Sun closed; free), which focuses on the flora and fauna of the Mojave Desert.

The museum is centrally located on the campus of the University of Nevada – Las Vegas (UNLV), which lies around 2 miles (3km) east of the Strip. If driving, the simplest way to get there from the Mirage is to drive south on the Strip for about one mile (2km) to East Harmon Avenue, which ends in the middle of the campus, turning south at Gym Drive. The museum is right there. Inside are exhibits on Nevada's wildlife, and artifacts created by American Indians.

UNLV Arboretum

The university's "arboretum" is a series of gardens throughout the campus, including native plant collections as well as a rose garden, an AIDS memorial garden, and a pool designed to attract birds, with a shaded viewing area.

Las Vegas Zoo

Can't get enough animal viewing? Las Vegas does have a small zoo, the Southern Nevada Zoological and Botanical Park, located about 15 minutes' drive northwest of the Strip (1775 Rancho Drive; tel: 702-647-4685). Besides every species of poisonous reptile that lives in Nevada, the zoo's biggest draw is the only family of Barbary apes in the US.

Lunch

By now it should be around 2pm. If you fancy lunch, a good option for healthy eating is the **Veggie House**, see ②, around 4 miles (6km) northeast of the UNLV campus on Spring Mountain Road. After lunch, return to the Strip by driving directly west along West Flamingo Road. If you do not want to stop for refreshment at this point, head straight back to the Strip by continuing south on Gym Drive to East Tropicana Avenue and turning right.

FLAMINGO WILDLIFE HABITAT

The route now continues by exploring nature attractions at a number of other large casino hotels, starting with the modest, beautifully landscaped island off the main lobby of the **Flamingo Las Vegas** ❸ (3555 Las Vegas Boulevard South; tel: 702-733-3111; www.flamingolv.com; see also pages 30 and 88). This island is home to a flock of Chilean flamingos, as well as numerous Asian pheasants, swans, ducks, parrots, turtles, and koi.

LION HABITAT RANCH

Formerly at the **MGM Grand** (see ③), these 40 magnificent creatures thankfully now live on **Lion Habitat Ranch** ❹ (382 Bruner Avenue; tel: 702-595-6661; Mon–Fri 11am–4pm), a dedicated 8.5-acre ranch, around 20 minutes' drive south of the Strip near the M Resort Spa Casino and Saint Rose Parkway,

Mandalay Bay Shark Reef

MANDALAY BAY SHARK REEF

If the lions have given you a taste for sharp-toothed carnivores, **Shark Reef** at the **Mandalay Bay Hotel** ❺ (3950 Las Vegas Boulevard South; tel: 702-632-7777; www.mandalaybay.com; daily 10am–11pm) should appeal. To get there, continue south for another two blocks, where the Mandalay Bay Hotel's 22ft (7 meter) -deep aquarium is one of the largest in the US, with 1.5 million gallons (5.5 million liters) of salt water.

To bring the tour full circle, consider heading back to the Mirage for dinner at **Cravings**, see ❹, which does one of the better all-you-can-eat buffets on the Strip.

Food and Drink

❶ PARADISE CAFÉ

Mirage Hotel, 3400 Las Vegas Boulevard South; tel: 702-791-7111; daily 24 hours; $$

Enjoy the serene sounds of the waterfall and savor classic dishes. Whether you're in the mood for a refreshing cocktail or a lavish lunch, this poolside café is the perfect retreat from the Strip. Start your day in paradise with a light breakfast or take a break from swimming to order a guest favorite like the Ice Chichi, Mirage's signature cocktail, served in a coconut.

❷ VEGGIE HOUSE

5115 Spring Mountain Road; tel: 702-431-5802; www.veggiehousevegas.com; daily 11am–9.30pm; $$

All-vegetarian Chinese stir-fries and noodles are served in a low-key setting with an indoor gazebo. This relatively new eatery has become something of a cornerstone in the Las Vegas community and has been recognized for its outstanding Chinese cuisine, excellent service, and friendly staff.

❸ RAINFOREST CAFÉ

MGM Grand, 3799 Las Vegas Boulevard South; tel: 702-891-8580; daily 11am–11pm; $$

Kids love this jungle-shrouded restaurant with its waterfalls, artificial trees, and animatronic gorillas and elephants. The large, predictable family dining menu features cute names – Safari Salads, Passport to Paradise Pizza, Galapagos Seafood Pasta, Congo Catfish, and so on. Desserts include a Sparkling Volcano brownie sundae big enough for two kids (or about six adults) to share.

❹ CRAVINGS

The Mirage, 3400 Las Vegas Boulevard South; tel: 702-791-7111; Mon–Fri 7am–9pm, Sat–Sun 8am–9pm; $$$

The buffet at Cravings features international gourmet cuisine from 11 cooking stations, including Asian, Mexican, Italian, and Japanese. The buffet also includes free beer and wine refills. Decor is sleek and modern. Expect a long wait in line at this long-time Vegas favorite.

Mural dedicated to Hunter S. Thompson, Fremont Street

3

ARTISTIC LAS VEGAS

Until recently, Las Vegas was notoriously lacking in cultural sophistication. While there is still little of the performing arts, paintings are another matter and the city is emerging as one of the top art destinations in the Southwest.

DISTANCE: 7 miles (11km) to the 18b Arts District and back
TIME: Around 4 hours (allow extra time if you are also doing breakfast, dinner and a show)
START/END: The Venetian/ Bellagio or Wynn Las Vegas
POINTS TO NOTE: Reservations are advisable for breakfast at Bouchon and must be made far in advance for dinner at Picasso should you choose to eat there. Guided tours for the Neon Museum are available by prior booking only. This tour is best done by car or taxi.

In 1998, when billionaire developer Steve Wynn announced that he would display works from his world-class art collection in his elegant new hotel, the Bellagio (see pages 39 and 86), and charge admission to see them, other casino owners scoffed. The displays, though, were an immediate hit and because they were open only to hotel guests, they attracted the wealthiest clientele on the Strip. Today, the thoroughfare has no fewer than three major art museums, and galleries and artists' studios have proliferated throughout the city.

THE VENETIAN

We suggest starting with an early breakfast at the **Bouchon**, see ①, in the **Venetian** ❶ (3355 Las Vegas Boulevard South; tel: 702-414-6200; www.venetian.com; see page 85). This will set you up nicely for a stroll through the **Grand Canal Shoppes** (Sun–Thu 10am–11pm, Fri–Sat 10am–midnight), the Venetian's shopping mall, with its *trompe-l'oeil* sky fresco, detailed building facades, singing gondoliers, strolling vendors and street performers, which all seems worlds apart from the Las Vegas glitz outside.

The **Regis Galerie** (tel: 702-414-3637; www.regisgalerie.com), which will be of special interest to art connoisseurs, carries Fabergé eggs, tabletop bronze sculptures, gemstone globes, *giclées* (high-quality reproductions of artwork)

The Neon Museum

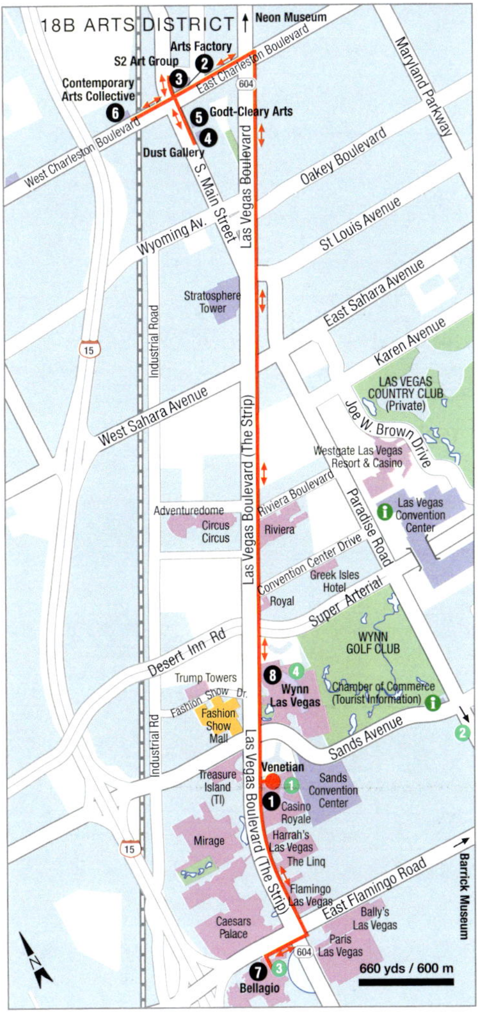

18B ARTS DISTRICT

Neon Museum
Arts Factory
S2 Art Group
Contemporary Arts Collective
Godt-Cleary Arts
Dust Gallery
East Charleston Boulevard
604
West Charleston Boulevard
Maryland Parkway
Oakey Boulevard
S. Main Street
Las Vegas Boulevard
Wyoming Av.
St Louis Avenue
Stratosphere Tower
East Sahara Avenue
15
Industrial Road
Karen Avenue
LAS VEGAS COUNTRY CLUB (Private)
West Sahara Avenue
Las Vegas Boulevard (The Strip)
Joe W. Brown Drive
Westgate Las Vegas Resort & Casino
Riviera Boulevard
Paradise Road
Adventuredome
Circus Circus
Riviera
Las Vegas Convention Center
Convention Center Drive
Greek Isles Hotel
Royal
Super Arterial
WYNN GOLF CLUB
Desert Inn Rd
Trump Towers
Fashion Show Dr.
Fashion Show Mall
Wynn Las Vegas
Chamber of Commerce (Tourist Information)
Sands Avenue
Industrial Rd
Treasure Island (TI)
Venetian
Sands Convention Center
Casino Royale
Harrah's Las Vegas
The Linq
Mirage
Flamingo Las Vegas
East Flamingo Road
Barrick Museum
Caesars Palace
Bally's Las Vegas
Paris Las Vegas
Bellagio
660 yds / 600 m
N

and more. Other galleries in the Grand Canal Shoppes include Peter Lik's, the Lumas, and the Wyland Signature Gallery.

NEON MUSEUM

The next stop is a few miles away from the Strip toward Old Town and Fremont Street. The outdoor Boneyard of the **Neon Museum** (770 Las Vegas Boulevard North; tel: 702-387-6366; www.neonmuseum.org), located in the city's Cultural Corridor, is not only an international tourist destination, but also a beloved project and collection for the Las Vegas community. The collection of electronic artwork goes back to the 1930s and tells the unique story of this famous city that blossomed in the desert. All that's often left of Vegas's past is the sculptural metal and neon, arranged in this gravel lot on Las Vegas Boulevard. Guided tours are available by prior booking only and appointment times are determined by availability of staff.

Barrick Art Museum

BARRICK MUSEUM

Once a natural history museum, the **Barrick Museum** (4505 South Maryland Parkway; tel: 702-895-3301; www.barrickmuseum.unlv.edu; Mon–Wed, Fri 9am–5pm, Thu 9am–8pm, Sat noon–5pm; free), on the University of Nevada's Las Vegas campus, has now changed its focus to art in an attempt to fill the void left when the Las Vegas Art Museum closed its doors in 2009. The staff at Barrick provide and maintain interesting exhibitions for the whole community to enjoy, while raising funds for the museum's development at the same time. Shows have ranged from contemporary paintings and sculpture, to a photography exhibition documenting legendary photographer Ansel Adams's black-and-white works of American landscapes and architecture, covering a period of 50 years.

18B ARTS DISTRICT

By now it should be early afternoon. If you're hungry, the **Origin India** (see ②) is just around the corner from the Barrick Museum. After a bite to eat, it is time to explore the other side of the Las Vegas arts scene, at the **18b Arts District**. (Readjust your schedule if you are fortunate enough to be in town for the district's First Friday festivities – see below.)

The 18b Arts District got its name when the city declared this run-down 18-block area between the Strip and Downtown to be its official art studio zone. Still dominated by car repair shops and used furniture stores, it doesn't look like much unless you know which doors to peek behind – except during the monthly event, **First Friday**, which sees all the studios in the district throw open their doors for receptions and other local artists display their work in the streets. Not surprisingly, it has become a major celebration, attracting as many as 15,000 visitors between 5 and 11pm.

Arts Factory

At other times of the month, highlights of the arts district include the **Arts Factory** ❷ (101–7 East Charleston Boulevard; tel: 702-383-3133; www.theartsfactory.com; opening hours vary, call or visit website for details). The *de facto* center of this creative melting pot, this old brick warehouse with its exterior mural commemorating the city's gay and lesbian community appears abandoned until you enter through the black westside door and go upstairs. Here, you'll find around 15 small studios that share space with a graphic arts firm and an architect.

S2 Art Group

Another highlight of this area is the **S2 Art Group** ❸ (1 East Charleston Boulevard; tel: 702-868-7880; www.s2art.com; opening hours vary, call or visit

Fiori di Como

Bellagio Gallery of Fine Art

website for details). The former lithographer for Norman Rockwell, Jack Solomon, moved his studio in 1991 from New York to Las Vegas. Jack passed away in 2012, aged 83, and several artists now use his former flatbed presses, and you can often watch them at work in this storefront space next to the Arts Factory.

Other commercial galleries

Also in the 18b Arts District, **Dust Gallery** ❹ (1221 South Main Street; tel: 702-880-3878; www.dustgallery.com; Wed–Sat noon–5pm) represents local and national painters and sculptors; and the large **Godt-Cleary Arts** ❺ (1217 South Main Street; tel: 702-452-2000; www.gcarts-lv.com; Tue–Sat 10am–6pm) exhibits works by big-name New York artists, both past and contemporary.

Not too far away, and worth a look if you are keen on art by living artists, is the **Contemporary Arts Collective** ❻ (231 West Charleston Boulevard; tel: 702-382-3886; www.lasvegascac.org). One of Las Vegas's oldest galleries, it is a non-profit co-operative showcasing contemporary sculpture, painting and mixed-media work by many of the city's top artists. Formerly part of the Arts Factory, the collective now occupies the ground floor of the new Holsum Lofts, an historic building that was originally a bread factory.

At this point, we suggest returning to your hotel or the Strip by retracing the route to cool off, rest up, and get dressed for dinner.

BELLAGIO GALLERY

Whenever the subject of art in Las Vegas comes up, somebody is sure to mention the **Bellagio** ❼ (3595 Las Vegas Boulevard South; tel: 702-693-7871; www.bellagioresort.com; see pages 45 and 86), about three blocks south of the Venetian and across the street. Former owner Steve Wynn took most of his art collection with him when he sold the Bellagio, and today the hotel's **Bellagio Gallery of Fine Art** (Sun–Thu 10am–6pm, Fri–Sat 10am–9pm) displays temporary exhibits that are curated by major Southwestern universities.

Recent exhibitions have included photography by Ansel Adams and ceramics by Pablo Picasso. Call the hotel or visit the website for details of current shows. Even if it does not appeal to you, a visit to the Bellagio is certainly worthwhile, if only to see *Fiori di Como*, the spectacular 2,000-sq-ft (186-sq-meter) field of colorful blown glass flowers that is American glass artist Dale Chihuly's crowning achievement, which spans the lobby ceiling.

EVENING OPTIONS

Suggestions for dinner include staying at the Bellagio for a meal at the **Picasso**, see ❸, if you have reser-

Jeff Koons' Popeye at the Wynn

vations, or heading down the Strip to Wynn Las Vegas, for a less formal meal at **Wynn Buffet**, see 4, and – if you are in the mood for further activities and culture – art and a show at the Wynn Las Vegas hotel.

Steve Wynn's Picasso

The show *Le Rêve* was named after Steve Wynn's favorite Picasso painting, a blue-period portrait of the painter's 21-year-old mistress, Marie-Thérèse Walter. Wynn had also originally planned to use the title as the name for his new hotel. He had bought the Picasso in 1997 for a whopping $48.4 million. Nine years later, a Las Vegas legend started when he agreed to sell it to another collector for $139 million – the highest price ever paid for a painting. The story goes that a day after Wynn signed the contract, but before the sale was completed, he was showing the painting to guests, including television journalist Barbara Walters and screenwriter Nora Ephron, at a cocktail party in his penthouse. Wynn, who claims to lack peripheral vision because of a medical condition, gestured at the painting – and poked a 6-in (15cm) tear in it with his elbow. Wynn's comment, according to Ephron, was: "Oh, shit, look what I've done. Thank God it was me." Lloyds of London, insurer of the painting, settled with Wynn for an undisclosed amount in April 2007, and he has since announced that he does intend to get the painting restored.

WYNN LAS VEGAS

For the latter option, taxi down the Strip to the towering **Wynn Las Vegas** 8 (3131 Las Vegas Boulevard South; tel: 702-770-7000; www.wynnlasvegas.com; see page 85), home to Steve Wynn's art collection. After the sale of the Bellagio, Wynn eventually moved the bulk of the paintings he had originally exhibited there to his new hotel, where he tried to charge an even steeper entrance fee. Because of sluggish ticket sales, he closed the exhibit in 2006 and hung many of the paintings, including works by Turner, Van Gogh, Vermeer, Gauguin, Matisse, and Warhol, around the common areas of the hotel, where you gaze upon them while you wait for *Le Rêve* to start.

Le Rêve

A blatant attempt to beat the Cirque du Soleil Company (see pages 55 and 59) at its own game, *Le Rêve* (French for "The Dream") was conceived by Cirque's former creative director, Franco Dragone. Using multi-level pools of water instead of a stage, the theater-in-the-round production (tel: 702-770-9966; shows start at 7pm and 9.30pm) features acrobatics, swimmers, live music, birds and special effects (such as rain, snow, and fire). It mesmerizes audiences with scenes that are by turns whimsical, surreal, and nightmarish.

Le Reve

Food and Drink

1 BOUCHON

Venetian Hotel, 3355 Las Vegas Boulevard South; tel: 702-414-6200; www.venetian.com; Mon–Thu 7am–1pm, Fri–Sun 7am–2pm and 5–10pm daily; $$$

This French bistro at the top of the Venezia Tower, with an *alfresco* dining area surrounded by gardens as well as an indoor picture-window area, is ranked by many food critics as one of the finest casual gourmet restaurants in America. Diners can savor bistro classics including *Poulet Rôti* (roast chicken) and *fruits de mer* (seafood) but breakfast here is much more affordable, and the ambience is the same. Breakfast items range from a basket of French pastries to an elaborate version of baked eggs Florentine over wilted spinach with *jambon au poivre* (peppered ham) and *boulangère* potatoes simmered in beef-onion stock. Besides the usual breakfast juices and beverages, you can order fresh strawberry milk or an espresso martini.

2 ORIGIN INDIA

4480 Paradise Road; tel: 702-734-6342; www.originindiarestaurant.com; daily 11.30am–10.30pm; $

This no-frills authentic Indian eatery is just around the corner from the Barrick Museum and serves up some dynamite low-budget lunchtime specials. Trust me when I say quality, authentic Indian food is often hard to come by in the US; this is a rare find.

3 PICASSO

Bellagio Hotel, 3595 Las Vegas Boulevard South; tel: 866-259-7111; daily 5.30pm–9pm, closed Tue; $$$$

This elegant French-Mediterranean restaurant, designed as a tribute to Pablo Picasso by his son Claude, is decorated with original Picasso paintings valued at $50 million, making the $100-plus price of a four-course prix-fixe meal or a five-course chef's *dégustation* menu seem like a bargain. (Just remember that many Las Vegas visitors lose far greater sums at the casino tables in less time than it takes to dine here.) A typical meal might include poached oysters garnished with caviar; shrimp with roasted pears; breast of pheasant with morel mushrooms; and the dessert of the day. A bonus is the fabulous view of the lake in front of the hotel, where hundreds of fountains dance to music every half-hour during the afternoon and every 15 minutes after dark.

4 WYNN BUFFET

Wynn Las Vegas, 3131 Las Vegas Boulevard South; tel: 702-770-3340; daily 8am–10pm; $$–$$$

Another good bet – and more affordable than the Picasso – is the chic buffet at the Wynn Las Vegas. Filled with flowers and white wicker, the decor alone is enough to set this dining room apart from other gourmet all-you-can-eat venues on the Strip. The amazing array of foods includes 17 active cooking stations offering everything from thick steaks to sushi and Alaskan king crab legs to down-home country-fried chicken.

The front desk at the Paris Hotel

4

INTERNATIONAL VEGAS

Built in 1966, Caesars Palace was the first of the city's themed casinos that married American-style glitz and excess with international cultural references. After Vegas's fortunes dwindled in the 1980s, a new breed of casino emerged, heralding the age of the megaresort.

DISTANCE: 4 miles (7km), plus an optional 2-mile (3km) detour for lunch
TIME: Around 5.5 hours, not including lunch, dinner or show
START: Paris Las Vegas Hotel
END: Mandalay Bay (or Wynn Las Vegas if you end with the suggested dinner, or New York New York if you end with the suggested show)
POINTS TO NOTE: The tour is done on foot or monorail, with a taxi necessary for the lunch option. If you do want to see Cirque du Soleil (the recommended show), ensure you book well in advance (see pages 46 and 117).

In the 1980s, Las Vegas's economic and population growth rates slumped to one-sixth of what they had been during the 1950s and '60s. Part of the reason may have been that organized crime funding dried up, but the biggest factors were probably the legalization of gambling in Atlantic City in 1976 and federal court rulings that opened the door to Native American casinos in 1979. Gambling was no longer enough to draw tourists to this isolated desert outpost. Opportunity awaited the developer who could figure out how to keep the town from drying up and blowing away.

That developer was Steve Wynn, who parlayed his part-ownership in a downtown casino as well as using his contacts with billionaire Howard Hughes and junk-bond magnate Michael Milliken into a deal to build the world's most expensive hotel. That hotel was the Mirage, the prototype for the huge megaresorts that fill the southern Strip today.

International theme park

Improbable as it seemed, the "If you build it, they will come" approach worked so well that within a decade, more than a dozen of the world's largest destination hotels had sprung up along a 1-mile (2km) stretch of Las Vegas Boulevard South, distinguished from one another by themes that paid tribute to various nations of the world. Together, they formed a single international theme park, much like Disney's Epcot Center in Orlando but on a much grander scale.

Paris Hotel *Arc de Triomphe and the Eiffel Tower at Paris Las Vegas*

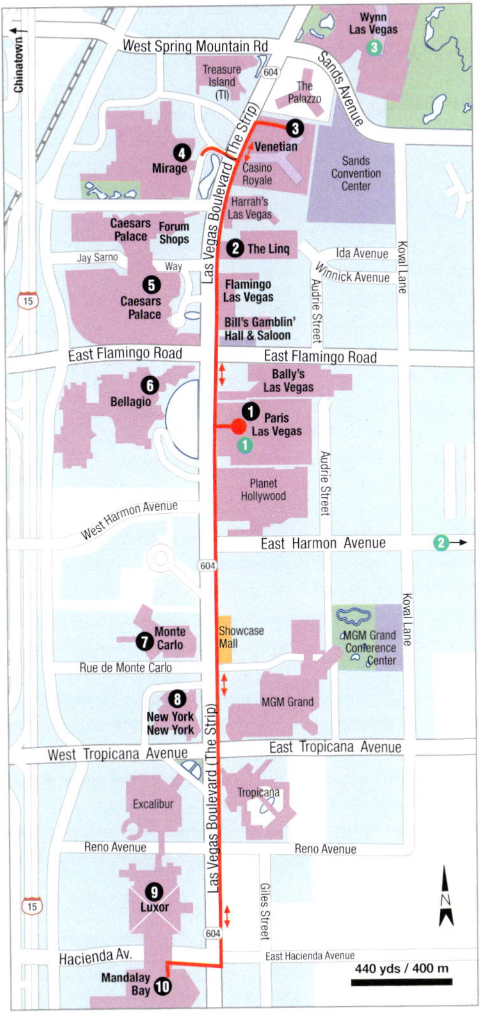

Today, the most popular pastime for Las Vegas visitors is wandering this section of the Strip to "see the world" in a day.

PARIS LAS VEGAS

Since the lunch recommendation on this itinerary is off-Strip, non-drivers may wish to simplify their day by filling up at the all-you-can-eat breakfast buffet at **Le Village Buffet**, see ①, at **Paris Las Vegas** ❶ (3655 Las Vegas Boulevard South; tel: 702-946-7000; www.parislasvegas.com; see page 91) and then just choose another lunch stop. On the Strip, you are never more than about 100ft (30 meters) from food, so there are plenty of options and alternatives.

GLOBAL VIEW

North of Paris Las Vegas, many of the themed hotels are on the west side of the street and you can get a helpful overview by walking along the east side first to see them from a dis-

Gondola rides in the Venetian

tance. Head past **Bally's** (see page 85), **Bill's**, the **Flamingo** (see pages 30, 34, and 88), **Jimmy Buffet's Margaritaville** eatery and the **Harley-Davidson Café**, and you'll also pass the **Linq** ❷ (3535 Las Vegas Boulevard South; tel: 800-634-6441), a hotel resort complex that opened in 2014, built on the site of the aging Imperial Palace.

THE VENETIAN

Now continue along the Strip to the breathtaking **Venetian** ❸ (3355 Las Vegas Boulevard South; tel: 702-414-1000; www.venetian.com; see pages 36 and 85). It is a reigning monarch among the Vegas destination resorts, where the two main attractions are **Madame Tussauds** and the **Grand Canal Shoppes** (Sun–Thu 10am–11pm, Fri–Sat 10am–midnight). The latter is one of the most impressive of the international hotels' malls, with its gondolas, *trompe-l'oeil* and floodlit sky, street performers, living statues, all set in a grand-scale replica of St. Mark's Square in Venice.

THE MIRAGE

Cross the Strip to the tropical-themed **Mirage** ❹ (3400 Las Vegas Boulevard South; tel: 702-791-7111; www.mirage.com; see pages 44 and 84), the megaresort that started it all. When the Mirage first opened, it drew huge crowds of curious spectators from the very beginning. Within three years, the casino was the biggest money-maker on the Strip. Even though the hotel needed to take more than a million dollars a day to break even, it never seemed to be a problem. Today, the crowds still come for the lush rainforest entrance, tropical ambience and white tigers – not to mention the volcano in front of the hotel. Its shopping mall, the Street of Shops, is designed to resemble an exclusive European shopping boulevard.

CAESARS PALACE

Two blocks south is the Ancient Rome-themed **Caesars Palace** ❺ (3570 Las Vegas Boulevard South; tel: 866-227-5938; see pages 65 and 86), which reigned as the city's most opulent resort from the time its doors opened in 1966, until the completion of the Mirage 23 years later. It has kept pace over the years, expanding to five times its original size, and remains one of the Strip's most impressive megaresorts.

Forum Shops

Giant Roman columns, mosaic floor patterns and outsized reproductions of Classical Roman sculptures make exploring this resort fun. In particular, check out the **Forum Shops** (Sun–Thu 10am–11pm, Fri–Sat 10am–midnight), a labyrinth of upscale designer boutiques that are among the most exclusive in the US.

Caesars Palace statue

Hofbräuhaus

BELLAGIO

Continue another block south to the **Bellagio** ❻ (3600 Las Vegas Boulevard South; tel: 888-987-6667; www.bellagio resort.com; see pages 39 and 86), styled after the town of the same name on Lake Como, Italy. The hotel's best-known attractions include its **Gallery of Fine Art** (see page 39) and the spectacular fountain show performed in the "lake" in front of the hotel at frequent intervals from mid-afternoon until midnight. Especially worth a visit is the **Conservatory and Botanical Gardens** (daily 24 hours; free) just off the main lobby, where exotic plants and flowers create a riot of color, fragrance, and shape.

MONTE CARLO

Two more blocks south, on the same side of the road, is the more affordably priced sister hotel to the Bellagio, the **Monte Carlo** ❼ (3770 Las Vegas Boulevard South; tel: 888-529-4828; www.montecarlo.com; see page 90). The two are usually connected by a tram, but it is advisable to call beforehand to check the link is working. Although the Monte Carlo has no real sightseeing attractions of its own, the casino is worth a peek because of its lavish decor, which is inspired by the place du Casino in Monte Carlo, Monaco. The hotel is a convenient place to catch a taxi if you're going out to the Germanic **Hofbräuhaus**, see ❷, for lunch. (If you are driving, head up either East Harmon Avenue or East Tropicana Avenue, both of which intersect with Paradise Road.)

NEW YORK NEW YORK

Back on the Strip, continue your tour at **New York New York** ❽ (3790 Las Vegas Boulevard South; tel: 866-606-7111; www.nynyhotelcasino.com; see page 74 and 90), an amazing homage to the Big Apple, with residential towers designed to look like skyscrapers and a casino styled on Central Park, complete with trees. You'll also find replicas of the Statue of Liberty and Brooklyn Bridge, and a Coney Island-style amuse-

Chinatown

The American Southwest has had a sizeable Chinese population ever since laborers came here to build railroads in the late 19th century. However, Las Vegas has only had a well-defined Chinatown since 1995, when a Taiwanese developer built Chinatown Plaza (Spring Mountain Road at Valley View Boulevard), which has enticed many Asians to move to Las Vegas and open businesses here. Three other major Asian shopping centers have opened in the same area and Chinese residents are the fastest-growing ethnic group in Las Vegas today, accounting for about five percent of the population. The Chinatown area is also home to many Filipino, Vietnamese, Japanese, and Korean communities.

Excalibur

ment center, complete with its own rollercoaster.

LUXOR

Next stop, another couple of blocks south and past the Disney-castle-style **Excalibur** (see page 88), still on the same side of the Strip, is the shining black pyramidal **Luxor** ❾ (3900 Las Vegas Boulevard South; tel: 702-262-4000; www.luxor.com; see page 89). One level up from the casino floor, you enter the world's largest atrium, with 29 million sq ft (3 million sq meters) containing all of the resort's restaurants, shops, and theaters.

Formerly at the Luxor, the King Tut exhibition can now be found at the **Las Vegas Natural History Museum** (900 Las Vegas Boulevard North; tel: 702-384-3466; daily 9am–4pm). This precise replica of the tomb of Egyptian Pharaoh Tutankhamun was created from the notes of British archaeologist Howard Carter, who discovered the actual tomb in 1922. The museum contains replicas of the gold sarcophagus, chariot, guardian statues, and hundreds of other objects found in the tomb, all reproduced by hand using the same tools and 3,300-year-old techniques. The 15 minutes visitors are allowed to view the exhibit is not nearly enough time.

MANDALAY BAY

Next door to the Luxor, the large, showy, gold-hued **Mandalay Bay** ❿ (3950 Las Vegas Boulevard South; tel: 702-632-777; www.mandalaybay.com; see pages 35, 58 and 89) has a nebulous Southeast Asian concept apparently inspired by Rudyard Kipling's poem *Mandalay*, though there is no bay anywhere near the actual landlocked town of Mandalay, Myanmar (formerly Burma). No matter. The Mandalay Bay's real theme seems to be an imaginary tropical paradise, replete with artificial foliage and waterfalls as well as strange statues of fantastical creatures such as earless unicorns and musical frogs. Asian visitors note the resemblance to new casinos in Macau, the semi-autonomous administrative region of China, where several Las Vegas gaming corporations – including the Mandalay Bay's parent company, MGM Mirage – are building lavish new resorts. Look out for the Eye Candy bar, with its cool bright lights.

DINNER

To continue the international theme at the end of the tour, a good choice for dinner would be the **Mizumi**, see ❸, at Wynn Las Vegas (see pages 40 and 85). The hotel is at the northern end of the Strip, so possibly best reached by taxi, if your energy is starting to flag.

CIRQUE DU SOLEIL AT NEW YORK NEW YORK

Representing a whole host of different nationalities, Cirque du Soleil has

The Luxor and Mandalay Bay

been part of Las Vegas for more than 20 years. Their 90-minute shows run all year long, and have everything from music to illusion and from acrobatics to artistry. Cirque du Soleil is a Canadian entertainment company from French Quebec; the name means Circus of the Sun and each performance is an unforgettable Las Vegas event, with a show to suit every taste and age group. Fun, energy, sensuality, and excitement take to the stage at eight world-class theaters at New York New York (3790 Las Vegas Boulevard South; tel: 866-606-7111; www.nynyhotelcasino.com; Fri–Tue 7pm and 9.30pm).

Food and Drink

1 LE VILLAGE BUFFET

Paris Las Vegas Hotel, 3655 Las Vegas Boulevard South; tel: 702-967-4859; daily 7am–10pm; $$

Unlike other hotels' broadly international buffets, this one is unusual in that the food is almost all French. Fill up on crêpes, pastries, sausages, cheeses, fruit, and much more. Delicious coffee, too. Savor it all in various dining settings that reflect different kinds of French provincial architecture.

2 HOFBRÄUHAUS

4510 Paradise Road; tel: 702-853-3227; www.hofbrauhauslasvegas.com; Sun–Thu 11am–11pm, Fri–Sat 11am–midnight; $$–$$$

Located one mile (1.5km) east of the Strip, the Hofbräuhaus is the city's only major German-themed establishment. This vast restaurant and beer garden, with its 45ft-high (14 meter) ceiling (complete with murals), is a lookalike franchise owned by the 400-year-old brewery of the same name founded by the Duke of Bavaria in Munich, Germany. It features imported Hofbräuhaus beer, an Oktoberfest atmosphere, and authentic German foods like Sauerbraten, a Bavarian pot roast, and Riesen Fleischpflanzerl, a sort of pork-and-beef hamburger.

3 MIZUMI

Wynn Las Vegas, 3131 Las Vegas Boulevard South; tel: 702-248-3463; Sun–Thu 5.30–10pm, Fri–Sat 5.30–10.30pm; $$–$$$$

Chef Devin Hashimoto, named "Best chef on the Strip" by Vegas Seven, has a fresh approach to Japanese cuisine and offers a choice of dining experiences at Mizumi: a robatayaki bar, a teppanyaki room, ocean-fresh sushi, and sashimi. Located at Wynn, the award-winning restaurant looks out over private Japanese gardens surrounding an idyllic koi carp pond with a shimmering 90ft (27-meter) waterfall. Experience the picturesque view and stylish, fine-dining approach to the delicious theatrics of teppanyaki presented in the teppan room.

Circus Circus

LAS VEGAS WITH KIDS

While Sin City is no longer branding itself as a family-friendly destination, it does have diversions that are suitable for children. Teenagers might find suitable attractions a little thin on the ground though...

> **DISTANCE:** 2 miles (3.2km) for the afternoon tour plus 2 miles (3km) for the dinner show
> **TIME:** Around 4 hours (tour only)
> **START/END:** Circus Circus
> **POINTS TO NOTE:** For this route, take the bus (CAT route 108; free for five-year-olds and under), a taxi or drive. Reservations are recommended at the Buy tickets up to 60 days in advance for the Tournament of Kings show.

For a few years in the 1990s, Vegas tried to promote itself as a family destination. Though it never amounted to serious competition for Orlando in Florida, it did draw a lot of parents with kids in tow, and often acted as a gateway for trips to the Grand Canyon and other Southwestern vacation hot spots.

There was just one problem. By law, children aren't allowed to gamble: casinos rake in a lot more money than rollercoasters, so image shapers did an abrupt U-turn to revive the old Sin City image with their now-familiar "What happens in Vegas..." pitch. Still, kids love the lights and over-the-top spectacle, and the amusement rides on offer just keep getting better and better.

CIRCUS CIRCUS

Start the day with breakfast at the child-friendly **Circus Circus** ❶ (2880 Las Vegas Boulevard South; tel: 702-734-0410; www. circuscircus.com; see page 84), at the **Circus Buffet**, see ①.

Adventuredome

At around 10am, head for Circus Circus's **Adventuredome** (summer: daily 10am–midnight). This domed complex is said to be America's largest indoor amusement park, though at 5 acres (2 hectares) it isn't as big as it sounds like it should be and the rides slot together like puzzle pieces to make the most of the space. Rides include thrill rides such as the Canyon Blaster – a double loop, double corkscrew rollercoaster (riders must be at least 4ft or 122cm tall) – and

Ride at the Adventuredome

Horse game in the Adventuredome

the El Loco, where riders ascend 90ft (27 meters) before dropping over and under to experience 1.5 vertical-Gs. There are also bumper cars, a swinging pirate ship, and tame junior rides to keep the little ones happy.

Circus acts and midway

Also at Circus Circus are performances by trapeze artists, tightrope walkers and other daredevils (daily 11am–midnight; free); extraordinarily, these take place at regular intervals high above the casino floor, with a safety net to protect the slot machine players from falling performers. The best vantage point for watching both the circus acts and the gamblers is from the mezzanine, much of which serves as a carnival-style midway with ball-throwing games and other feats of skill you can play to win stuffed toys and similar prizes. The midway also has a number of child-oriented shops such as Nothing But Clowns, Sweet Tooth, and Circus Kids.

Spiderman at Madame Tussauds

LUNCH

At around 12.30pm, it is time to move on from Circus Circus by walking along Riviera Boulevard to cross the Strip. Keep on walking (if it is just too hot, or the kids are too hungry, hop in a cab) for one block, until you reach the **Westgate Las Vegas Resort & Casino** ❷ (3000 Paradise Road; tel: 888-796-3564; www.westgatedestinations.com), home to **Sid's Café**, see ②, which is our recommendation for lunch.

Alternatively, you can continue along the Strip (catch the CAT route 108) to the **MGM Grand** (3799 Las Vegas Boulevard South; tel: 702-891-1111; www.mgmgrand.com; see page 89), and then have lunch at the hotel's **Rainforest Café** (see page 35) if you prefer a more natural kind of theme, although it'sa bit of a detour.

Magicians

Las Vegas has even more magicians than Elvis impersonators. A family favorite (and easy on the wallet) is Mac King, who performs afternoon shows at Harrah's (3475 Las Vegas Boulevard South; tel: 702-369-5222; Tue–Sat 1pm, 2pm, 3pm, 4pm). Quirky and comical, King is best known for his "amazing goldfish trick," catching live fish over the heads of the audience on a fishing line baited with Fig Newtons.

Some of the less traditional Las Vegas magic acts are less suitable for children: Penn and Teller's show at the Rio All-Suites Hotel and Casino is billed as family-friendly, though moms of younger kids may not appreciate the spurting blood illusions.

WAXWORKS

In the mid-afternoon, head back to the Strip along Riviera Boulevard, and bus down it to the **Venetian** ❸ (3377 Las Vegas Boulevard South; tel: 702-862-7800; www.venetian.com; see pages 36 and 85) for **Madame Tussaud's Interactive Attraction** (daily 10am–10pm). This pricy museum contains more than 300 life-sized, uncannily realistic wax figures of celebrities and historical figures, from George Washington and Abraham Lincoln to the Dalai Lama, Julia Roberts, and Britney Spears. It is "interactive" because you are invited not only to touch the figures, but also have your photograph taken, posing with Siegfried & Roy and their famous white tiger, singing along with Elvis Presley or playing golf with Tiger Woods. It's educational, too – after a certain fashion.

Alternatively, or in addition to the waxworks, you may want to see if you can take a **gondola ride** (Sun–Thu 10am–11pm, Fri–Sat 10am–midnight) along the hotel's "Grand Canal." Reservations must be made in person, on the same day only.

Tournament of Kings

EVENING SHOW

Our recommended show for the evening is the *Tournament of Kings* at **Excalibur** ❹ (3850 Las Vegas Boulevard South; tel: 702-597-7600; shows Wed–Mon 6pm, 8.30pm; see page 88), which is further down the Strip (just past the MGM Grand). There are two showings a night (except Tue), so, depending on whether you want to go for the early or late one, you can either head directly there or you can fit in a short rest at your hotel beforehand.

Tournament of Kings

This 75-minute dinner extravaganza features nonstop action, with jousting knights, swordfights, horse races, pyrotechnics, and general uproar, as audiences cheer their combatants on, based on which area of the hall they are sitting in.

The medieval theme carries over to the tasty banquet fare, served just before the show starts. Starting with "dragon's blood" (tomato soup), you also get a whole roast Cornish game hen with potato, vegetables, non-alcoholic beverages and dessert. But you don't get silverware. In true Dark Ages fashion, you dine with your fingers.

HOTEL OPTIONS

Both Circus Circus and Excalibur are excellent choices if you are visiting Las Vegas with children. Children under the age of 12 and accompanied by an adult stay for free at Excalibur and Circus Circus. Needless to say, those who aren't visiting with kids may prefer to stay somewhere else, where the average age of guests is rather higher!

Food and Drink

❶ CIRCUS BUFFET

Circus Circus, 2880 Las Vegas Boulevard South; tel: 702-734-0410; Mon–Fri 7am–2pm, 4.30–10pm; Sat–Sun 7am–4pm, 4.30–10pm; $

This is one of the largest and lowest-priced all-you-can-eat buffets on the Strip and its long waiting line moves fairly fast. While it has been upgraded recently, some locals still avoid it because of its questionable quality in the past. The food is aimed specifically at children's tastes – crunchy, gooey, greasy, and syrupy sweet.

❷ SID'S CAFÉ

Westgate Las Vegas Resort & Casino, 3000 Paradise Road; tel: 888-796-4564; Sun–Thu 7–10pm, Fri–Sat 7–midnight; $–$$

Sid's Café offers a creative approach to home-style cooking, as well as attentive service and large plates of freshly prepared food. Menu options include appetizers, salads, diverse entrées, delicious burgers and desserts. Try the Elvis Sandwich in the very resort he once called home in Las Vegas. Visit Sid's Cafe and experience what it's like to be treated like a high roller!

Indoor skydiving

THRILL-SEEKERS' LAS VEGAS

It used to be that the casino floor provided all the excitement a visitor to Vegas could want. But now speed, heights, and adventures in Cyberspace also make the heart beat faster – and prices will take your breath away, too.

DISTANCE: 3.5 miles (5.6km) plus monorail ride
TIME: A full day
START: Flyaway Indoor Skydiving
END: New York New York (or MGM Grand if you end with the suggested show)
POINTS TO NOTE: Buy an all-day pass for the monorail. Reserve well ahead for MGM Grand's Kà.

Gambling has always been an effective way for Las Vegas visitors to get their adrenaline racing. But today, the Strip offers many other state-of-the-art experiences that rival the top rides in any of the world's best amusement parks (and some cost more, too). Even jaded vacationers who find slot machines and roulette boring will get their fill of sudden rushes in this itinerary. By the end of the day, you'll be ready to head for the casino just to relax and take it easy! By the way, do not drink until dinner: tickets for most of the activities on this itinerary won't be sold to you if alcohol can be detected on your breath or demeanor.

INDOOR SKYDIVING

Let your breakfast digest properly before you start with some indoor skydiving at **Flyaway Indoor Skydiving** ❶ (200 Convention Center Drive; tel: 702-731-4768; www.flyawayindoorskydiving.com; daily 9.45am–8pm; please note under-18s must be accompanied by an adult; no sandals or open-toed shoes are allowed, and no persons the management considers obese will be permitted to ride).

The experience

If you've never tried skydiving before, this is an uncannily realistic way to simulate the experience. If you have, this three-minute ride lasts longer than the real thing usually does. You are given 20 minutes of live and video instruction on how to fly and land, then a DC-3 propeller blasts you up into a 22ft (7-meter) vertical wind tunnel, simulating a 120mph (190kph) free fall.

Ride on the Stratosphere Tower

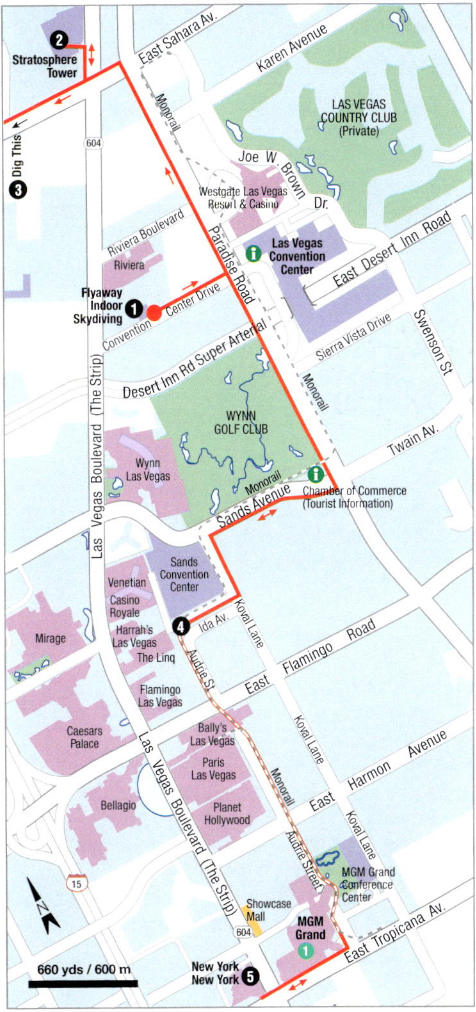

Unlike actual skydiving, though, you don't have to worry about whether your parachute will open – because you're not wearing one. Expensive, yes, but this truly is a once-in-a-lifetime opportunity to experience flying, Superman-style.

SKYDIVING FOR REAL

If you want the real McCoy, make arrangements through Skydive Las Vegas (tel: 702-759-3483; www.skydivelasvegas.com) or Las Vegas Skydiving Center (tel: 702-303-3914; www.lasvegasskydivingcenter.com). All offer beginners' lessons, tandem free falls (where an instructor holds you), and even skydiving weddings.

STRATOSPHERE TOWER

The only thing missing from Flyaway is the view of the ground rushing up at you from far below. For that, take a short cab or bus ride down to the north

Dig This

end of the Strip, and the **Stratosphere Tower** ❷ (2000 Las Vegas Boulevard South; tel: 702-383-5210; Sun–Thu 10am–1am, Fri–Sat 10am–2am; riders must be at least 4ft 6in/137cm tall). Without a doubt, this is where you'll find the most shocking thrill rides on the Strip. The observation tower near the top of the tallest structure in Las Vegas (1,149ft/ 350 meters) commands a jaw-dropping 360-degree view of the city and the surrounding mountains and desert, and the high-speed glass elevator up to the indoor and outdoor observation decks is a thrill in itself.

Three rides

The three rides off the observation decks are the highest (above ground level) amusement-park-style rides in the world. The **Big Shot** shoots you up a 160ft (49-meter) tower in 2.5 seconds, registering up to 4Gs in the process, before drifting weightlessly back down. Or there's **Insanity**, which seats you at the end of a 64ft (19-meter) arm that spins you outward at an angle of 70 degrees with nothing between you and the Strip nearly 100 stories below. The scariest of the three rides, though, is **X Scream**. You enter an eight-passenger car that hoists you to the top of a 27ft (8-meter) arm and then the car drops you over the edge of the deck and downward, jerking to a sudden stop in mid-air. The experience is sure to bring alive your most basic nightmare of falling.

DIG THIS

Not many people know about this one. And it will be probably one of the coolest things you've ever done. Located northwest of the north end of the Strip, past the Venetian, is a "heavy equipment playground" where thrill-seekers can drive life-size bulldozer toys for fun. Seriously. You can choose either a burly Caterpillar D5G bulldozer or a 315CL hydraulic excavator. With a bulldozer, you can build huge mounds and push gigantic tires; with an excavator, you can dig trenches, and stack 2,000-pound (900kg) tires. Or you can even try both.

Called **Dig This** ❸ (3012 South Rancho Drive; tel: 702-222-4344; daily 10am–3.30pm), it's just the other side of the Las Vegas freeway from the Strip, so it's a short drive away. There's an in-cab orientation and an instructor will show you the working of each little button and lever so that you can move your machine with grace and poise. Something that's not easy to do at first. The classroom time is essential, but not overbearing, and the machines are well maintained. They're also air-conditioned, which is something you'll be grateful for in the Nevada sunshine.

MONORAIL

After lunch, it's time for a trip on the Las Vegas **monorail** ❹ (tel: 702-699-

KÀ at Cirque de Soleil

8200; www.lvmonorail.com; Mon–Thu 7am–2am, Fri–Sun 7am–3am), which you can board at Harrah's/The Linq Station, which is south of Sands Avenue. Follow the monorail track down Koval Lane for a block and turn right down Krueger Drive and the station is a short walk. The ride south to the end of the line takes you past all the hotels on the east side of the Strip, offering a quick tour of megaresorts such as the Venetian, Paris Las Vegas and, at the end, the MGM Grand, from two stories above sidewalk level.

MANHATTAN EXPRESS

At the MGM Grand, hop off the monorail and walk west along Tropicana Avenue to cross the Strip and reach **New York New York** ❺. The facade – a copy of the New York skyline – is impossible to miss. Outside, the **Manhattan Express** (Sun–Thu 11am–11pm, Fri–Sat 10.30am–midnight) is the original Strip resort rollercoaster; it careers at speeds up to 67mph (108kph) along the hotel roofline and above replicas of skyscrapers, the New York Harbor and the Statue of Liberty. The 3-minute ride features two drops of more than 100ft (30 meters), a unique 180-degree heartline twist and dive, and a 540-degree spiral.

EVENING SUGGESTIONS

One option for the evening is the **MGM Grand**, where you can have dinner at **Emeril's New Orleans Fish House**, see ①, and then catch the show by **Cirque du Soleil** (tel: 702-531-3000 or 866-740-7711; Sat–Wed 7pm and 9.30pm), which makes for a suitably breathtaking end to this thrill-seeking day. In the show, entitled *Kà*, the action is played out on a five-story-tall stage with a floor that raises from horizontal to vertical in mid-performance. Barbarian pirates swing across the theater on ropes and shoot flaming arrows over the heads of the audience. Sinking ships, young lovers, bursts of fireworks, strange languages, swordfights, and, of course, the most unbelievable acrobatics add up to an unforgettable entertainment experience.

Food and Drink

① EMERIL'S NEW ORLEANS FISH HOUSE

MGM Grand, 3799 Las Vegas Boulevard South; tel: 702-891-7374; www.emerils.com; daily 11.30am–10pm; $$$

Whether it is scallops from Maine, pike from the Midwest, or redfish from Texas, celebrity chef Emeril Lagasse "kicks it up a notch" with Creole-Cajun flair in a setting that is more Bourbon Street than the Strip. The house special, New Orleans barbeque shrimp, is especially tasty. Meat and chicken dishes are also available.

Hilton Lake Las Vegas

ROMANTIC LAS VEGAS

Vegas is a magnet for romantics who favor a different type of scene. Be it elopement, engagement, honeymoon, commitment vows, marriage or illicit affair – Las Vegas loves lovers.

DISTANCE: 40 miles (64km)
TIME: A full day (including dinner and show)
START: Hilton Lake Las Vegas
END: Mandalay Bay (or Stratosphere Tower if you end with the dinner suggestion, or New York New York if you end with the show suggestion)
POINTS TO NOTE: There are several things to organize in advance with this tour: make spa reservations as far ahead as possible and buy Zumanity tickets weeks in advance; make reservations (timed for sunset) at the Top of the World two weeks or more in advance; and arrange limousine rental at least one day before you plan to do the tour. "Smart-casual" dress, meaning a jacket for men and no jeans and trainers, is required for our dinner recommendation.

Las Vegas boasts less than half a percent of the US population, yet it is the location of choice for five percent of all the country's marriage ceremonies. And although it is actually statistically quite rare for couples who have come to Vegas just for fun to get drunk and wake up to find themselves unexpectedly married, myths of this kind are certainly the stuff of American comedy and cheesy films. That would never happen to you, of course, but the mere possibility adds a special tingle to romance in Las Vegas. Regardless, whether you're pondering the idea of taking your partner home to meet the folks; or you've already bought the ring in anticipation of the perfect moment to pop the question; or you have just noticed what a great smile your spouse of 20 years has, when such a moment comes along, spare no expense.

HILTON

Breakfast in bed is a wonderful way to start a romantic day, and for a particularly lovey-dovey time, spend the night outside of Sin City at the **Hilton** ❶ (Lake Las Vegas; 1610 Lake Las Vegas Parkway, Henderson; tel: 702-567-4700; www3.hilton.com). Don't count on a lie in here though, as a clock tower nearby starts chiming from 7am and golfers,

Ethel M's Chocolate Factory and Botanical Gardens at Christmas

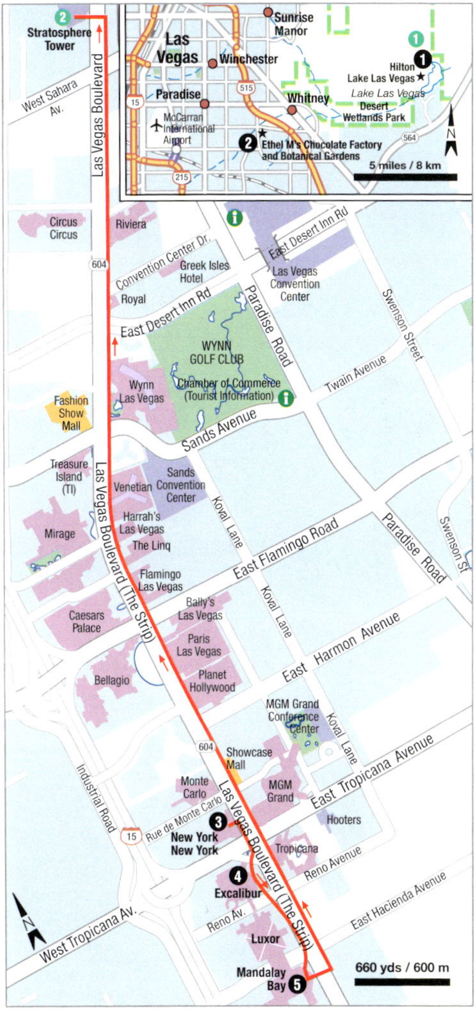

who make up a large part of the hotel's clientele, tend to get up early in the morning and make noise in the hallways. Just call room service, which can serve you such tantalizing breakfasts as baked malted waffles with caramelized pineapple.

Lake Las Vegas

After breakfast, head outside to the man-made **Lake Las Vegas**. If you are not staying at the Hilton, this is the best place to start the tour. There's a paved public walkway around the lake and the Hilton has its own sandy beach, with kayaks and bicycles available to rent for guests. The more ambitious will find hiking trails running from the hotel into the surrounding vast, empty desert. In summer, the early morning sun warms the dry air fast: by 9.30, it may drive you back inside the air-conditioned hotel. Another option is a visit to the nearby MonteLago 'village' resort with its quaint, cobblestone streets lined with chic shops.

Enjoying the view from the Top of the World Restaurant

Spa

If you are hungry, head back to the hotel for a bite at the **Poolside Bar & Grill**, see ❶. Follow this with a spot of relaxation in the whirlpool by the waterfalls, then drip in the steam room, and simmer in the sauna. There are separate facilities for men and women, but the spa has treatment rooms for couples. Hot stone massage, aromatherapy massage, and a full menu of other body-healing pleasures are available to couples for an additional $25 above the regular price. You can also lounge together on the spa's sundecks and in the garden.

CHOCOLATE TOUR

After lunch, it is time to head off to **Ethel M's Chocolate Factory and Botanical Gardens** ❷ (12 East Ogden Avenue; tel: 702-383-3340; www.ethelschocolate.com; daily 9am–10pm; free). The chocolate factory is north of the Strip, up toward Fremont Street.

Scientists may not yet have proven that chocolate is unquestionably an aphrodisiac, but you can certainly investigate for yourselves by visiting this premier gourmet chocolate maker for a self-guided factory tour (including free samples), and a stroll in the desert gardens with their spiky cacti.

CAVIAR AND VODKA

Continue into central Las Vegas and park your car (if driving) at the casino at **New York New York** ❸ (3790 Las Vegas Boulevard South; see also pages 45, 74, and 90); leave it there until you are ready to return to your hotel. Cross the street to the **Excalibur** ❹, where you can catch the free monorail tram past the Luxor to the **Mandalay Bay** ❺ (3950 Las Vegas Boulevard South; tel: 702-632-7777; see also pages 35, 46, and 89). Your first destination is **Red Square**, the hotel's Russian-themed restaurant and bar, which has more than 100 kinds of premium vodka chilling in its freezer vault. Fur coats and hats are provided for the sub-zero temperatures. When you enter the vault, you find the bar is made of solid ice, providing a fantastic contrast to the desert heat outside the hotel.

EVENING OPTIONS

If this has set you up for a memorable dinner, our suggestion for an unforget-

Tasting Room at Ethel M's Chocolate Factory

Zumanity

table meal out is the Stratosphere Tower's **Top of the World Restaurant**, see ❷, (also see page 54), although to get there, you need to head all the way down the Strip. One option for this is to hire a stretch limo – all those you see cruising up and down the Strip are for rent by the hour. If you make arrangements well in advance, you can have one waiting for you at the Mandalay to take you to the restaurant. Or, just take a taxi down the Strip and order a limousine to pick you up after your meal.

These limos are as luxurious inside as most hotel rooms, with built-in televisions, sound systems, minibars, and sofa-style seats that wrap around the interior. You'll probably have a one-hour minimum rental, so have the driver cruise up and down the Strip to pass the time.

Zumanity at New York New York

After dinner, head back to **New York New York** at the southern end of the Strip if you want to continue the themed tour with the 10.30pm showing of *Zumanity* (tel: 702-740-6815 or 866-606-7111; shows Tue–Sat at 7.30pm and 10.30pm; over 18s only).

Of the five Cirque du Soleil shows on the Strip, this one is by far the most sensual, blending burlesque, cabaret, acrobatics, and special effects with a few naughty bits. The atmospherically lit show includes seductive versions of traditional circus skills such as contortion and aerial stunts, along with dance styles that range from flamenco and tango to African dance, Viennese waltz, and even striptease, making it a fitting end to this romantic tour.

Food and Drink

❶ POOLSIDE BAR & GRILL

Hilton Lake Las Vegas; 1610 Lake Las Vegas Parkway, Henderson; tel: 702-567-4700; www3.hilton.com; mid-spring–mid-fall 11am–10pm; $$

Cool off in the pool, then dine while you dry (towels are not essential in the desert sun). This café serves sandwich wraps, salads, smoothies and other healthy fare, as well as festive drinks.

❷ TOP OF THE WORLD RESTAURANT

Stratosphere Tower; 2000 Las Vegas Boulevard South; tel: 702-380-7777; daily 11am–11pm; $$$

There are few places as romantic as a revolving restaurant, and the Las Vegas Strip has one of the best. Perched 800ft (244 meters) in the air on the tallest structure on the Strip, this restaurant revolves 360 degrees every 80 minutes. Time your reservations to coincide with sunset for the take-your-breath-away experience of watching the Strip light up before your eyes. It is so fabulous it can even overshadow the menu, which features delicacies like lobster and crab ravioli, Muscovy duck and Colorado rack of lamb. Try the Chocolate Stratosphere filled with mouthwatering Belgian chocolate mousse for dessert.

Red Rock Canyon Road

8 OLD WEST LAS VEGAS

Go off the beaten track and you will find that Vegas has history, too: this all-day adventure reveals the Las Vegas Valley's pioneer years as an oasis for farming and ranching in the harsh Mojave Desert.

DISTANCE: 65 miles (105km)
TIME: A full day
START: Golden Gate Hotel
END: Larry's Hideaway
POINTS TO NOTE: This route is best done by car, preferably an air-conditioned one. Make an early start, heading off by 9.30am, earlier if possible. If you want to do a sunset trail ride in Red Rock Canyon (note that this is fairly expensive), book as far ahead as you can.

Las Vegas became a railroad town when it was chosen as a stopping point for trains. Then, cowboys came to the saloons on Fremont Street for much the same kind of recreation that is offered by casinos to visitors today. As you spend time Downtown, you'll no doubt see authentic Westerners from Montana, Wyoming, and Idaho towns, where most commercial flights from the local airports go to Las Vegas, as well as many who make their homes in the vast, mostly empty landscape that surrounds Sin City.

GOLDEN GATE HOTEL

If you want an Old West-style hotel, try the **Golden Gate Hotel** ❶ (1 Fremont Street; tel: 702-385-1906 or 800-426-1906; www.goldengatecasino.com; see page 92). Make an early start with breakfast at the hotel's **Du-Par's Restaurant & Bakery**, see ①.

OLD LAS VEGAS MORMON FORT STATE PARK

From the hotel, follow North Main Street northeast to Washington Avenue; turn right and drive about four blocks to the intersection with North Las Vegas Boulevard and **Old Las Vegas Mormon Fort State Park** ❷ (500 East Washington Avenue; tel: 702-486-3511; http://parks.nv.gov/parks/old-las-vegas-mormon-fort; daily 8am–4.30pm), the first main stop of the tour.

Old Mormon Fort

Within the park is one of Nevada's most venerable buildings, the Old Mormon Fort, which was built to protect mis-

Old Las Vegas Mormon Fort

sionaries and settlers en route to California. Inside the high adobe walls, a reconstructed tower overlooks a plaza deserted except for a broken-down wagon and the iron pegs for throwing horseshoes.

The only surviving part of the original structure is the building nearest to the little creek, rising from underground aquifers a few miles west. These supplied a water source running through the fort, nourishing the poor soil in which the hopeful missionaries planted crops, including potatoes, tomatoes and squash. Some of these same plants are grown today in the museum's demonstration garden.

After the Mormons left, a miner named Octavius Gass acquired the site, along with other land, to assemble a sizable ranch – the first in the region. He also opened a general store and blacksmith shop. It was then bought by Archibald Stewart, whose widow Helen ran the ranch after her husband was killed in 1884, and later sold the property to the railroad. The site on which the Stewart home stood is scheduled for excavation to unearth any secrets that may lie buried beneath.

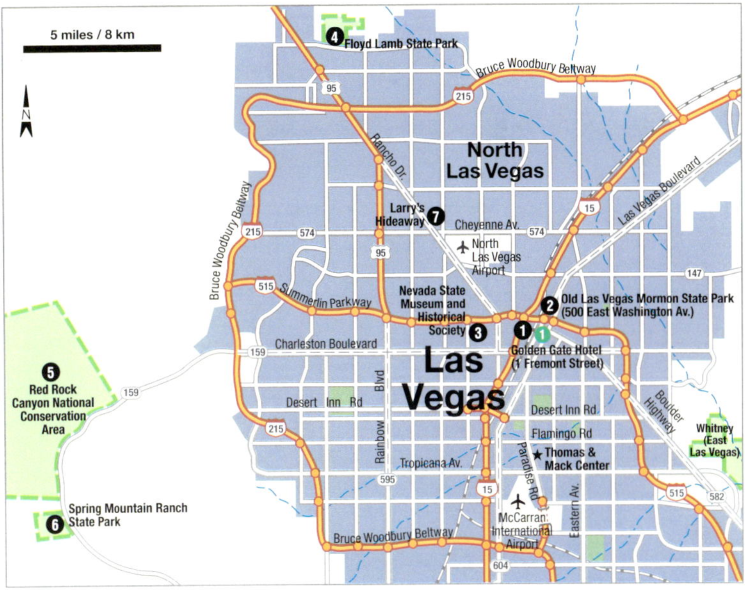

Nevada State Museum

NEVADA STATE MUSEUM AND HISTORICAL SOCIETY

Next stop is the **Nevada State Museum and Historical Society** ❸ (309 South Valley View Boulevard; tel: 702-486-5205; http://museums.nevadaculture.org; Thu–Mon 10am–6pm). Until recently this small museum was set on a lake in Lorenzi Park, off Washington Avenue, 3 miles (5km) due west of the Old Mormon Fort, but in 2011 it moved to new premises fewer than 2 miles (3km) away, next door to the Las Vegas Springs Preserve on Valley View Boulevard, west of Downtown. Twice the size of its old home, this new museum showcases historical exhibits on the Las Vegas area from pioneer days through World War II, as well as fossils, and stuffed and mounted specimens of present-day Mojave desert fauna.

Pro Rodeo's "Superbowl"

The biggest cowboy event of the year in Las Vegas, the National Finals Rodeo, has been held at the Thomas & Mack Center in Las Vegas every December since 1985. The 10-day event draws upward of 140,000 spectators each year to watch the top professional rodeo athletes in the US and Canada compete in saddle bronc riding, bareback bronc riding, bull riding, calf roping, team roping, steer wrestling, and barrel racing. Tickets are very hard to get. A lottery is held one year in advance, and only one out of every 25 people who enter actually get tickets. There is a second lottery for balcony seating 10 months ahead. To try for a ticket, visit www.nfrexperience.com. Tickets are often available online from vendors who buy blocks of tickets to resell individually at a profit. First Choice Tickets (www.nfr-rodeo.com) and (www.vegastickets.com) are good places to start.

FLOYD LAMB STATE PARK

By now it should be around noon – time for a spot of lunch at the **Floyd Lamb State Park** ❹ at Tule Springs (9200 Tule Springs Road; tel: 702-229-8100; daily 9am–5pm). This is 15 miles (24km) north of downtown Las Vegas off US Highway 95 (take exit 93 – Durango Drive – and follow the signs). You can pick up picnic fixings near the park at Albertsons supermarket (8410 Farm Road; tel: 702-658-2030).

The park is named after the late state senator Floyd Lamb, who was instrumental in getting the land transferred to the state in 1977. Six years later, Lamb was convicted of soliciting a $20,000 bribe from an undercover FBI agent. Ever since then, the authorities have been trying to have his name removed from the park. As you may have guessed by now, they have been

Floyd Lamb State Park

Red Rock Canyon

unsuccessful in their efforts. Guided carriage tours are available within the park.

Historic site

This 2,040-acre (825-hectare) park occupies the site of Tule Springs, a large desert oasis that was a stopping place for nomadic Indian hunters and, later on, explorers and prospectors. Farmer Bert Nay bought water rights to the springs and started a small farm here in 1916. It was expanded into a working cattle ranch in 1941 and, during the late 1940s, it was converted into a dude ranch, where women stayed while establishing Nevada residency to take advantage of the state's liberal divorce laws.

The park today

Today, several buildings from the former ranch still remain, along with the descendants of the peacocks that strolled the lawns during the ranch's heyday. Most of the park is natural desert, with three fishing ponds (a Nevada fishing license is required if you want to fish) fed by the springs. Picnic tables with grills surround the ponds. The springs area is also known as one of Nevada's major fossil quarries, where remains of mammoths, giant camels, sloths, miniature horses and even giant condors have been found. Note that many of these fossils can be viewed at the **Las Vegas Natural History Museum** (900 North Las Vegas Boulevard; 702-384-3466; daily 9am–4pm).

RED ROCK CANYON

To reach **Red Rock Canyon** ❺ take Durango Drive to County Road 215 (also known as the Bruce Woodbury Beltway). Go south for 10 miles (16km) to exit 22, Charleston Boulevard/Red Rock Canyon. Follow West Charleston Boulevard (Nevada Highway 159) for 5 miles (8km) until you pass the Red Rock Canyon entrance (Scenic Loop Drive). Stay on the main highway for another 5 miles (8km), until you reach Spring Mountain Ranch.

Spring Mountain Ranch

The **Spring Mountain Ranch** ❻ (Red Rock Canyon National Conservation Area; 1000 Scenic Loop Drive; tel: 702-515-5350; tour times vary, so call ahead) dates back to 1876, when it was named Sand Stone Ranch. When the original owner died, he left it to two Paiute orphan boys whom he had adopted. The ranch later passed through the hands of several celebrity owners, including Hollywood furrier Willard George and the billionaire recluse Howard Hughes.

Guided and self-guided tours take in the original cabin, the mansion-like main house, the cemetery, the blacksmith shop, horse barn and corrals, and a facility where Willard George used to farm chinchillas.

Photographer in Red Rock Canyon

Cowboy Trail Rides

If your budget allows and you've booked well in advance, at around 5pm it is time for a sunset horseback ride and barbecue at Red Rock Canyon (Cowboy Trail Rides, Red Rock Canyon; tel: 702-387-2457; www.cowboytrailrides.com; hours vary; reservations essential).

A 90-minute guided horseback ride takes you through the narrows of Red Rock canyon floor, then up to Overlook Summit, where you can watch the sun set and the lights of Las Vegas come on in the distance. Then it's back to camp for a chuckwagon steak dinner, and, afterwards, you can roast marshmallows and s'mores (marshmallows with chocolate, sandwiched between wafers) over the campfire, listen to some tales and history, and sing along to cowboy songs.

If playing at cowboys does not appeal, head back into central Vegas and choose a restaurant from the Directory section of the guide (see page 94).

Cowboy threads

In Las Vegas, you can wear boots and a cowboy hat in the most exclusive resort hotels in town – including most restaurants that have dress codes – without feeling out of place. Visitors, both men and women, who find themselves in need of Western apparel will find great selections at Sheplers Western Wear (4700 West Sahara Avenue; tel: 702-258-2000) – the most conveniently located of three branches of Sheplers in Vegas – and Cowtown Boots (1080 East Flamingo Road; tel: 702-737-8469). During the National Finals Rodeo, more than 400 vendors sell Western wear at Cowboy Christmas, a public gift show held at the Las Vegas Convention Center.

LARRY'S HIDEAWAY

"Real" cowboys and cowgirls in the Las Vegas area go to **Larry's Hideaway** ❼ (3369 Thom Boulevard; tel: 702-645-1899; daily 24 hours), a huge country & western dance club with a small menu of bar food in an otherwise rather desolate area of north Las Vegas. To get here from Red Rock Canyon, retrace your route until you're going northbound on County Road 215. If you haven't heard any singing cowboys lately, be sure to come here on a Wednesday evening for karaoke night.

Food and Drink

① DU-PAR'S RESTAURANT & BAKERY

1 Fremont Street, Las Vegas; tel 702-366-9378; www.dupars.net/store; daily 24 hours; $$

A family-run chain that opened its first restaurant in 1939, Du-Par's arrived in Las Vegas back in the 1950s. They claim to have introduced the shrimp cocktail to Las Vegas in 1959, and to have served over 40,000,000 since. The food is classic and hearty. Try the buttermilk pancakes.

Caesars Palace slots

GAMBLERS' LAS VEGAS

Lured by Lady Luck, gamblers are glued to the slot machines whatever the time of day – or night. Here, we demystify the casino experience and introduce the range of gaming distractions on offer, for example, at Caesars Palace.

DISTANCE: N/A – the whole day is spent at Caesars Palace
TIME: Around 7 hours for the casino tour and free lessons
START/END: Caesars Palace
POINTS TO NOTE: The first free lesson is at 11am, but it is best to arrive early (say 10am) if you want to sit at the table instead of watching from the sidelines.

For serious gamblers, a trip to Las Vegas requires no detailed itinerary. Simply check into your favorite hotel – most likely a Downtown hotel, where there are fewer touristic distractions than on the Strip. Then head directly to the casino's cashier cage, invest in a tray of chips, and you're on your way.

But Las Vegas visitors who are new to the world of casino gambling often arrive with daydreams of breaking the bank. Maybe you have a special $20 bill that came from some friend or relative who asked you to bet their birth date at the roulette table. The reality is, first-timers usually lack the confidence to test their luck at casino tables and, instead, settle for a few not-very-exciting hours of watching their stake dribble away a quarter at a time in slot machines. Here is a painless plan to help you fathom the world of casinos. (For more gambling tips, see page 20.)

BREAKFAST AND A TOUR

Start with breakfast at around 9am. If you're at **Caesars Palace** (3570 Las Vegas Boulevard South; tel: 702-731-7110 or 800-634-6661; www.caesars.com; see pages 44 and 86), a good place is the **Café Americano**, see 1.

In Caesars Palace, or any other Las Vegas gaming hotel, visitors will have no problem finding the casino. It will be centrally located, so much so that you have to make your way through it to reach the reception desk, the swimming pool, the restaurants, the front door, or even the elevator to your room. Caesars Palace has three casino areas, totaling 149,000sq ft (13,845sq meters), surrounding the oldest of the hotel's guest room towers.

Playing the slots

SLOT MACHINES

The first thing you'll notice is that the casino is full of slot machines, the most popular casino games by a wide margin. A recent survey by the owners of Caesars Palace revealed that 66 percent of men and 81 percent of women play the slots rather than table games: they're simple, and you don't have to interact with a dealer or other players.

The odds

However, they also generally offer the worst odds in the casino. By Nevada state law, slot machines must pay out at least 75 percent of the money played in them, and most are programmed to pay out between 83 and 98 percent. But no matter how long you play, unless you hit the jackpot, the amount you win back will be a very small fraction of the amount you bet. What are your chances of hitting a jackpot? In the three years before this book was published, out of about 100 million visitors to Las Vegas, only five people won jackpots of $100,000 or more, with an additional four people winning jackpots over $1 million. It's the possibility, however slight, of winning a fortune that keeps people feeding all those "one-armed bandits." Caesars Palace encourages such notions by reminding patrons that they have paid out more million-dollar-plus jackpots than any other casino in the world. Of course, it has been operating for more than 40 years as one of the city's largest casinos, so this fact has nothing to do with your chances of hitting it big.

How to play

The slot machines in Caesars Palace accept bets in denominations from one cent to $500. The high-priced machines are located in separate, semi-private VIP areas. Many let you bet various amounts on the same machine. Try it. Find a quarter machine and feed a $10 bill into it. Pull the handle (or push the button – it makes no difference). A computer chip instantly picks a series of random numbers, then makes the whirling drums stop on the symbols corresponding to those numbers. Certain combinations mean you win. Nothing you can do, and nothing the machine has done before,

Slot machine

Craps board

will affect the outcome of the pull. Try it 39 more times, and you will have gambled the whole $10 bill once. Then cash out. (If you don't, the machine will let you keep going until you've lost all your credits.) Take the ticket the slot machine prints out to a cashier machine, which reads its bar code and gives you your money. Less than $10? Now you understand slot machines.

VIDEO POKER MACHINES

These, like other slot machines, work from a computer chip that generates random numbers and is programmed to a pre-set pay out percentage. Instead of offering pie-in-the-sky jackpots, they pay smaller amounts more frequently, and you can improve your odds through careful analysis. This doesn't mean you're any more likely to walk away a winner, but it does mean that if your real purpose is to keep the waitress bringing free drinks, you can study the screen endlessly, and play very slowly. If you need to brush up on your knowledge of poker hands – does a flush beat a straight? – video poker is the place to do it before moving up to other poker-based games like Caribbean stud or Pai Gow poker.

CRAPS

At most casino resorts, you can watch how-to-gamble lessons in your room on TV any hour of day or night, but they are no substitute for the actual experience of gambling on the casino floor. About two dozen resorts offer free table game lessons during the day, when the casino is not crowded. Caesars Palace offers lessons in five games at different times throughout the day (including at 11am, which fits in well with this tour; a second craps lesson at Caesars is daily at 5pm).

The odds

The polar opposite of slot machine gambling, craps, along with blackjack, offers players the best odds in the casino. It is also the most physical and extroverted; so many people are timid about trying it. The basic game is simple and depends entirely on chance. The betting layout is complicated, but you don't have to master it all. Many of the more complicated bets are "sucker bets," anyway. All you need to do is place your bet on the long, curved "pass line." In fact, you don't even have to know the rules – the dealer will either take your chip or give you another chip – but it's more fun if you understand the game.

When the person whose turn it is to shoot rolls the dice, if they come up 7 or 11 on their first roll, you win; if they come up 2, 3, or 12, you lose. If any other number comes up, it becomes the "point" that the shooter must roll again to win. However, if he or she rolls a 7 before their "point", then they lose ("craps out") and the dice are passed around the table to the next shooter. If you don't want to be a shooter, you can pass them along to the next person

Betting on roulette

ROULETTE

Roulette is the simplest of the casino's table games, which is why the free lesson (at noon) only takes 15 minutes. You can bet on one or more individual numbers, on clusters of numbers, or on whether the winning number will be even or odd, red or black. The dealer spins the roulette wheel, and whichever number the ball lands on wins. Because there are two extra numbers – "0" and "00" – the odds favor the house by about 5.3 percent. Roulette tends to appeal to people who believe in the intrinsic power of numbers or their own precognition.

BLACKJACK

Next up is blackjack, which is by far the most popular table game in Las Vegas casinos: more people play blackjack than all other table games combined. Caesars Palace offers free blackjack lesson daily at 12.15pm and 3.15pm.

How to Play

The rules are deceptively simple. You play against the dealer, placing your bet before the cards are dealt, and whichever player's cards total closest to 21, without going over, wins. The house advantage comes from the fact that one of the dealer's cards remains hidden until after you've decided whether to "twist" (take another card) or "stick." Rules about "doubling down" and "splitting pairs" let you raise the stakes on certain hands. A beginner can play blackjack after a few minutes of instruction; to play the game well takes practice in analyzing your chances based on the card the dealer is showing. Betting strategy is everything, and blackjack play can produce what seem to be phenomenal runs of luck, good or bad.

Now is the time, perhaps, to reflect on what you have learned so far over lunch at **Spago**, see 2. (Please note that even the fanciest restaurants in Vegas can speed you through, if required, so it will still be possible to fit a decent lunch in, despite the busy schedule of gaming lessons in this tour.)

RACE AND SPORTS BOOK

The race and sports book in Caesars Palace is one of the biggest and most spectacular in Las Vegas. Dimly lit, it has seating for 250 with seven big-screen television monitors – two of them 20 x 30ft (6 meters x 9 meters) in size. Smaller screens show all the major sporting events going on at the moment, and some seats have small plasma screens for watching horse races. A big electronic betting board displays the current odds on every pro sporting event coming up. You can bet on boxing, American football, basketball, baseball, golf, and hockey, auto racing, and horse racing. The rules for betting are different for various sports. Minimum bets are $10 for sports, $2 for races. Betting is not complicated, but

Roulette

Playing poker

information overload can be extreme. If you're not a seasoned sports betting buff, you might at least place a $10 bet on your team of choice.

POKER

Through a hallway from the race and sports book, there is the poker room, which has 30 tables. Few will be in use in the middle of the day; when night falls they will all be packed. Poker is the only Las Vegas casino game where gamblers play against each other, not the house. Besides the familiar Five-card draw, favorite games include Seven-card Stud, Omaha, and Texas Hold 'em; the last is by far the most popular live game in Vegas, and there are many tables at which this is the only game. At other tables games tend to alternate between the other different poker games. (As some cards in Texas Hold 'em are shared by all the players, it is hard to deal this and other games at the same table.)

Most poker tables have limits on how much you can bet or raise. Many professional poker players live in Las Vegas, and more fly into town every weekend. High-limit and no-limit tables are intended to attract pro play, leaving low-limit tables safer for casual players. If you play poker well and often back home, the poker room offers a chance to pit your skills against a table full of strangers and find out how good you really are. If you are a beginner, it might be safer to practice on the video poker games and watch the in-room television poker lessons first.

Pai Gow poker

Originally invented in the private poker clubs of California in the 1980s, Pai Gow poker is a hybrid version of *pai gow*, an ancient Chinese game played with domino-like tiles. (Caesars Palace is one of the casinos that also offers Pai Gow tables.) The poker version uses cards instead of tiles and poker hands instead of the original Chinese scoring combinations. You get seven cards,

Poker ploys

Regardless of status, motive, or method, most people make unconscious revelations through body language. In poker, this can be the difference between winning or losing. Tics, twitches, nervous laughs, or facial expressions are crucial giveaways. Having a "tell" can be a disadvantage and overcoming it is as difficult as changing any other unconscious personal habit: someone might be too quick to flip their cards if they have a good hand, or slump in their seat if they do not. Pay attention to the body language of your opponents and you might walk away with more money in your pocket than if you don't. A tip from one professional poker player is this: "Sit down at the table and spot the sucker. If you haven't made them within five minutes, get up and leave. Otherwise, the sucker is you."

Chips

which you divide into a five-card hand and a two-card hand. If both your hands beat the dealer's two hands, you win, and if both the dealer's beat yours, you lose. If you beat the dealer on one hand and they beat you on the other, it's a "push" (tie), and you keep your bet. Due to the large number of pushes, Pai Gow poker is a relatively slow-paced game, and you can play for hours without losing or winning huge sums. Try to catch the 2pm lesson.

MINI-BACCARAT

Baccarat, which dates back to the 15th century, is the favorite casino game in Monte Carlo and in many parts of Europe. Its popularity spread to America as part of the James Bond mystique, and today at most large Las Vegas Strip casinos, "big table" baccarat is played in a special roped-off area, or separate room where Arab sheikhs and Asian business tycoons bet astonishing sums on the turn of a card. Mini-baccarat is the same game, but it is played at a smaller table on the main casino floor. The betting limits are lower, and you don't have to dress up.

Mini-baccarat, just like baccarat, is entirely a game of luck. A single player competes against a banker to see whose hand comes closest to "9" (face cards count "0," aces count "1"). Everybody else at the table simply bets on whether the banker or the player will win the hand. Bets pay 2 to 1; you can also bet that the two hands will tie, which pays 9 to 1. In mini-baccarat, the dealer turns over both the banker's and the player's hands. Betting strategies are similar to blackjack, but playing skill is not a factor in baccarat as it is in blackjack. Mini-baccarat lessons are held at 4pm.

GARDEN OF THE GODS

If you are staying at Caesars Palace, and your head is reeling after a full day of learning about casino games, it's time to head for the pool for a little sunshine and relaxation. The exquisite 4.5-acre (2-hectare) **Garden of the Gods** swimming pool complex (daily Apr–Oct 8am–8pm, Nov–Mar 8am–6pm) is one of the best reasons to pick Caesars Palace as your hotel, since it is strictly for guests only. Lush gardens, tall palm trees, urns and Roman columns of Carrara marble surround four pools – one of which is designated specially for topless bathers – and two large whirlpool baths. The complex is said to be modeled on the ancient Roman baths of Caracalla, and has mosaics inspired by those at Pompeii.

DINNER AND GAMBLING

If you want to stay longer at Caesars Palace, consider dining at the **Old Homestead Steakhouse**, see ❸. Afterwards it is time to put your luck and learning to the test. Pick the action that appeals most to you and find a table that has an

Garden of the Gods

open seat, being careful to avoid the ones with high betting limits.

Place some cash on the table and the dealer will push it down a slot and give you chips in return. Although casinos will not honor each other's chips, all use the same color-coding system: red = $5, green = $25, black = $100. The dealer cannot redeem your chips or give change. At the end of the night, you have to go to one of the cashiers' cages to convert the chips back into cash. Remember, the odds always favor the house, so the law of probabilities guarantees that you will always lose if you play long enough. The secret to winning is to quit while you're ahead, which can be very hard to do. Many serious gamblers will limit their time at the tables to short intervals and take any sizable win as a cue to quit playing. Others will bet their whole stake on one turn of the card or spin of the roulette wheel, knowing that the likelihood of doubling their money is greater than if they spread smaller bets over a longer time.

People who gamble while their judgment is impaired by alcohol tend to lose much more. Notice the waitresses dressed in togas who circulate through the casino offering players free drinks? That's why. Good luck...

Food and Drink

1 CAFÉ AMERICANO

Caesars Palace, 3570 Las Vegas Boulevard South; tel: 702-650-5921; daily 24 hours; $–$$

Dig into an old-fashioned burger for lunch, made with Angus beef and topped with vine-ripe tomatoes, green leaf lettuce, Cabot Farm sharp white cheddar and a sesame brioche bun. Or try the Cuban sandwich, one of Café Americano's signatures.

2 SPAGO

Caesars Palace – Forum Shops, 350 Las Vegas Boulevard South; tel: 702-369-6300; daily 11am–11pm; $$$

Seasonal New American fare from Wolfgang Puck, served in sleek digs with a patio for people-watching.

3 OLD HOMESTEAD STEAKHOUSE

Caesars Palace, 3570 Las Vegas Boulevard South; tel: 702-731-7560; Sun–Thu 5–10pm, Fri–Sat 5–10.30pm; $$$$

A bit of East Coast steakhouse tradition is reinvented at Caesars Palace with the Las Vegas outpost of New York City landmark Old Homestead. Brothers Marc and Greg Sherry, whose family has been associated with the original Old Homestead (est. 1868) for decades, let Vegas get a taste of its fine cuts and legendary history. Complemented by sultry decor, dark woods and burgundy leather booths, Old Homestead's urban dining room and bar feels like a familiar favorite. (The glass wine cellar holding 15,000 bottles doesn't hurt, either.)

The Venetian

BUDGET LAS VEGAS

To find fun on the cheap – or even for free – in a place where money reigns supreme might seem a real challenge. However, in the hope of taking more from you than you are expecting to spend, the city has lots of bargains.

> **DISTANCE:** 4–5 miles (6–8km) for the daytime tour; 3–9 miles (5–14km) in the evening
> **TIME:** A full day
> **START:** SLS Hotel & Casino
> **END:** Fremont Street
> **POINTS TO NOTE:** Start early. The double-decker Deuce bus (a 2-hour pass costs $6, a 24-hour pass costs $8, and a 3-day pass costs $20) runs along the Strip and north to the Bonneville Transit Center (101 East Bonneville Avenue) every 6 to 15 minutes round the clock. Purchase a pass at a ticket vending machine (TVM).

Let's face it, Las Vegas is a bad place to be broke. Both the police and the resorts are notoriously intolerant of vagrants. For those who have lost all their money, the only realistic choice is to leave. But if you're a backpacker exploring America on a few dollars a day, or want to keep your spending for the casinos, the city does offer a lot to see and do on the cheap.

THE STRIP BY BUS

Start early, around 8am, and catch the double-decker Deuce bus up or down the Strip, depending on where you're staying. When you board, buy an $8 all-day pass. Get off at the **SLS Hotel & Casino** ❶ (2535 Las Vegas Boulevard South; tel: 702-761-7000; www.slslasvegas.com; see page 84), which is at the far north end of the Strip, amid the ghosts of former hotels that have been razed to make way for future condominium towers and resort complexes.

SLOTS-A-FUN

Walk down the Strip from SLS to this small casino next to Circus Circus. At **Slots-A-Fun** ❷ (2800 Las Vegas Boulevard South; tel: 877-849-4868) you can gamble almost for free. About half the slot machines take pennies or nickels. There is also nickel video poker, as well as $1 blackjack tables. Instead of free drinks, the casino offers donuts to players in the morning, and little sandwiches throughout the day.

Slots-A-Fun

Trapeze Show, Circus Circus

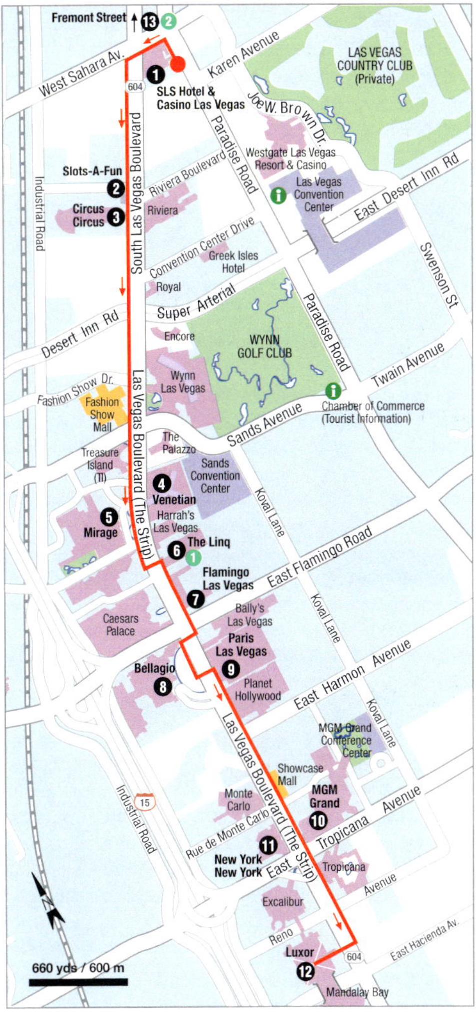

STRIP ATTRACTIONS

Continue strolling down the Strip from one air-conditioned resort lobby to the next. There are numerous free attractions along the way.

Circus Circus to the Venetian

On your right as you head down the Strip from Slots-A-Fun is **Circus Circus** ❸ (2880 Las Vegas Boulevard South; tel: 702-734-0410; see pages 48 and 84). Free attractions here include the extraordinary circus acts that take place above the casino floor.

Next, five blocks down on the left, is the **Venetian** ❹ (3355 Las Vegas Boulevard South; tel: 702-414-1000; see pages 50 and 85). Free highlights here include the Grand Canal and St. Mark's Square.

Mirage to the Flamingo

Opposite the Venetian, on your right, is the **Mirage** ❺ (3400 Las Vegas Boulevard South; tel: 702-791-7111; see pages 32,

Bellagio Conservatory

44, and 84), which marks the start of the southern stretch of the Strip. Without spending a dime here, you can marvel at the Siegfried and Roy Plaza, the lobby aquarium, and the tropical rainforest.

Walk back to the Strip, head down and cross over to the **Linq** ❻ (3535 Las Vegas Boulevard South; tel: 702-794-3174; see page 88). Here, you can visit the auto museum (Mon–Sat 10am–5pm; free). If you fancy some refreshment, look out for the **Yard House**, see ①.

Adjacent to the Linq is the **Flamingo** ❼ (3555 Las Vegas Boulevard South; tel: 702-733-3111; see pages 34 and 88). Stop by here to see the flamingo habitat.

Bellagio and Paris Las Vegas

One block farther on and on the other side of the road is **Bellagio** ❽ (3600 Las Vegas Boulevard South; tel: 888-987-6667; see pages 45 and 86). Time your walk so that you are at the lake in front of this hotel at 3pm, which is when the Strip's most spectacular free show, starring the Bellagio's choreographed fountains, takes place. It continues every half hour until dusk and runs every 15 minutes after dark. Next door, the volcano at the Mirage erupts during the evenings. Both of these are particularly impressive when viewed at night, should you wish to return on another occasion.

After you have admired the fountain show, head inside and see the conservatory and botanical gardens, again all at no cost.

Cross over the Strip again to reach **Paris Las Vegas** ❾ (3655 Las Vegas Boulevard South; tel: 702-740-7000; see page 91). Here, the architecture and decor are the highlights.

MGM Grand to the Luxor

On the same side of the road, just one block down, is the **MGM Grand** ❿ (3799 Las Vegas Boulevard South; tel: 702-891-1111; see pages 34, 50, and 89). Opposite is **New York New York** ⓫ (3790 Las Vegas Boulevard South; tel: 702-740-6969; see also pages 45, 58, and 90), remarkable for its architecture. The 47-story behemoth is Nevada's tallest casino at 529ft (160 meters) and its multiple facades are among the Strip's most visually exciting.

The world-famous Bellagio fountains

New York New York

Inside the Luxor

Finally, you reach the **Luxor** ⓬ (3900 Las Vegas Boulevard South; tel: 702-262-4000; see pages 46 and 89), where attractions include the inclined elevators (please note that these can only be ridden by guests) in the atrium, which is said to be spacious enough to accommodate nine Boeing 747s.

DOWNTOWN

From the southern end of the Strip, take the Deuce double-decker bus all the way to Downtown (see page 28). The bus makes frequent stops along the way. Our recommendation for dinner is the **Heart Attack Grill**, see ②, on **Fremont Street** ⓭.

Fremont Street Experience

Stay on Fremont Street for the centerpiece of Downtown's **Fremont Street Experience: Viva Vision** (daily 8pm, 9pm, 10pm, 11pm, and midnight; free). This spectacular sound and light show is projected onto the world's largest LED screen, a vaulted canopy that covers four blocks of the pedestrian-only Fremont Street, and has a 550,000-watt sound system. There are more than a dozen shows, and no show is presented twice in the same night. They range from *Lucky Vegas*, featuring classic Vegas icons, and *Speed, Smoke, and Spinning Wheels*, with an auto racing theme, to the extra-terrestrial *Area 51*, the psychedelic *The Drop*, and the sexy, adult-oriented, late-evening *Fahrenheit at Night*.

Food and Drink

① YARD HOUSE

The Linq 3545 Las Vegas Boulevard South; tel: 702-597-0434; www.yardhouse.com; daily 11am–1am (until 1.30am Fri–Sat); $$

The Linq Promenade is part of a recent initiative to shift some of the attractions of the Strip outdoors, but the best reason to visit here is a bar called the Yard House. It's actually a chain, with about 100 bars across the whole of the US, but don't let that fool you; this is one of the best bars you'll ever visit. It's big inside, but it's tasteful; it's modern, but maintains an elegant look and feel. The food here is excellent and there's a choice of literally hundreds of different craft beers, bitters, and ales on draft. There are TVs, but this isn't a sports bar. Even if you're not a particularly big beer drinker, there's enough choice here to tempt even the most tentative of palates.

② HEART ATTACK GRILL

350 Fremont Street; daily 11am–10pm; tel: 702-333-5555; $$

As the name suggests, this is a once-in-a-lifetime dining experience. The Heart Attack Grill offers a range of delicious burgers and hotdogs and then offers you the chance to double-up, triple-up, or, if you think your arteries can take it, customize your burger with eight meat patties. Punters must don hospital gowns to dine and are served by waitresses dressed as nurses.

LAKE MEAD AND THE VALLEY OF FIRE

Don't get so caught up in Las Vegas that you overlook what the surrounding area has to offer. Leave the themed tours behind and discover dramatic desert landscapes, ancient Indian art, and the largest man-made lake in the US.

DISTANCE: 134 miles (215km)
TIME: Around 5 hours
START/END: Las Vegas Strip
POINTS TO NOTE: This route is done by car and the mileage is heavy, so make sure you have a full gas tank and plenty of traction on your tires. As you will be heading through barren terrain, we do not recommend restaurants on this route, so please ensure you bring plenty of drinking water and snacks for the journey, along with sensible footwear. Aim to start by 6.30am if you want to escape the heat of the day in summer.

Few Las Vegas visitors take time to explore the desert wonderland that lies just a few miles the other side of Sunrise Mountain. It's a shame, because this natural, pristine landscape presents the perfect counterpoint to the traffic-clogged, over-the-top, artificial environment of the Strip. This open-road trip will add a new dimension to your Vegas vacation.

LAS VEGAS TO LAKE MEAD

In the summer months, you will want to start out as early as possible. From the Strip, take Tropicana Avenue east to Paradise Road and turn right. As you pass the airport, Paradise will merge into Interstate 215 and take you to **Henderson** ❶, 12 miles (19km) from the Strip.

Lake Mead by boat

The eastern shore of Lake Mead is not accessible by road, and most of the Colorado River arm of the lake cannot even be seen from any road. To explore the lake's hidden canyons, beaches, and inlets, you'll need a boat. Houseboats, as well as water skiing and fishing boats and personal water craft, are available for rent at Callville Bay Marina (100 Callville Bay Road; tel: 702-565-8958; daily 8am–6pm), 15 miles (24km) from the Henderson entrance station on a side road off Northshore Road, and at Echo Bay Marina (600 Echo Bay Road; tel: 702-

Shoreline of Lake Mead

394-4000), 35 miles (56km) from the Henderson entrance. We recommend reserving houseboats as far in advance as possible.

Beyond Henderson

The freeway ends at Henderson, and becomes Lake Mead Drive. Continue for 10 miles (16km), past the Lake Las Vegas resort complex, to the **Lake Mead National Recreation Area** ❷ entrance gate, where you must pay a small charge per car, which discourages joyriding by local teenagers and – except on weekends – usually means you'll have the road all to yourself. If you pass through the gate before the fee station is open, pay at the self-service kiosk. Go past the entrance and turn left onto Northshore Road.

NORTHSHORE ROAD

This scenic drive parallels the Lake Mead shoreline at a distance of about 4 miles (6km). For about half the way, the Black Mountains will block your view of the lake, but the desert, with its other-worldly landscapes of bare rock in hues of red, white, black, and tan thinly scattered with ocotillo, creosote, and datura plants will provide plenty for the eyes to feast on. Several roads turn off to the right, providing access to the lakeshore, including paved roads to the Callville Bay and Echo Bay marinas.

Hiking trails

Along the way are signs for the 2.5-mile (4km) Northshore Summit and Redstone Dune hiking trails. Another beautiful stop along this leg of the trip is **Rogers Warm Spring** ❸, a palm-fringed oasis with a crystal-clear pool teeming with small fish.

VALLEY OF FIRE STATE PARK

It's 46 miles (74km) and approximately a 90-minute drive (more if you stop en route) from

Sandstone formation at the Valley of Fire State Park

the Henderson entrance gate to the **Valley of Fire State Park** ❹ (tel: 702-397-2088; www.parks.nv.gov.vf.htm; park daily 6am–5pm; visitor center daily 8.30am–4.30pm). Nevada's oldest and largest state park encompasses an ancient red-and-white sandstone formation, uplifted and fractured by faults over the eons to form rock labyrinths and eerily eroded formations. Some of the cliffs are decorated with elaborate petroglyphs carved by nomadic American Indians 4,000 years ago. One of the best examples is high on the side of **Atlatl Rock**, reached by climbing a stairway from a picnic area on the scenic drive through the park.

For hikers, there is the fascinating half-mile (1km) trek to **Mouse's Tank**, said to have been the hideout of a legendary renegade Indian. Many species of birds and reptiles find shelter in the park, along with coyotes, foxes, skunks, tortoises, and jack rabbits. Hiking here is best done in the early morning, since it can be dangerously hot in the middle of the day. If you're one of the first hikers of the day in the sand-floored canyons, you will see the tracks left by hundreds of animals during the night.

LOST CITY MUSEUM

Located 8 miles (13km) north of the entrance to Valley of Fire along State Highway 169, the **Lost City Museum** ❺ (tel: 702-397-2193; http://museums.nevadaculture.org/lcm; daily 8.30am–4.30pm) preserves ruins and artifacts from Pueblo Grande de Nevada, the largest ancient Indian archeological site in the state, which was built by ancestral Pueblo people around AD 750 and thrived for 400 years before it was mysteriously abandoned. When its original location was about to be flooded by the creation of Lake Mead in the 1930s, the pueblo was taken apart, moved piece by piece, and reassembled at its present site in the improbably green farming town of Overton.

RETURN TO LAS VEGAS

The shortest route back to Vegas involves heading south from Overton to the Valley of Fire and driving through the park along Highway 169, which cuts an almost straight path for 25 miles (40km) across empty, eroded terrain. Join Interstate 15 at the corner of the Moapa Indian Reservation. This is the homeland of a small community of Paiutes, some of whom you may meet at the truck plaza near the Interstate 15 on-ramp.

From there, it is a quick and easy 33-mile (53km) trip back to town. The return trip from Valley of Fire takes about an hour; it is highly advisiable to ensure you are back in Las Vegas by late morning, as the midday sun can be unbearably hot.

Hoover Dam

HOOVER DAM AND GRAND CANYON WEST

Two of the most spectacular man-made wonders of the American Southwest (not counting Las Vegas itself), which were built 70 years apart, are found to the southeast of the city and can easily be visited in a single day.

DISTANCE: 246 miles (396km)
TIME: A full day
START/END: Las Vegas Strip
POINTS TO NOTE: This route is done by car and the mileage is heavy, so make sure you have a full gas tank and plenty of traction on your tires. As you will be heading through barren terrain, we do not recommend restaurants on this route, so please ensure you bring plenty of drinking water, snacks and lunch for the journey, along with sensible footwear. Aim to leave around 8.30am.

Completed in 1936 after five years of construction and a cost of $49 million and 104 workers' lives, the Boulder Dam (now known as Hoover Dam) was the most ambitious public works project of the Great Depression era. Spanning Black Canyon below the confluence of the Colorado and Virgin rivers, it created the largest man-made lake in the US, 110 miles (177km) long and some 500ft (152 meters) deep. After touring the dam, you can continue south to another, less utilitarian but equally dramatic, engineering feat built by the Hualapai Indians, which allows you to walk off the edge of the Grand Canyon.

LAS VEGAS TO THE HOOVER DAM

After a bright-and-early breakfast, leave Las Vegas following the same route described in the previous route through Henderson to the Lake Mead National Recreation Area entrance gate (see page 77). This time, continue straight after passing the gate to follow the Lakeshore Scenic Drive for 11 miles (18km), past Boulder Beach – a popular place to beat the heat on summer weekends – and the Las Vegas Boat Harbor. The road climbs up to join US Highway 93 just east of Boulder City. Then you begin a 3-mile (5km) switchback descent into Black Canyon to arrive at Hoover Dam.

HOOVER DAM

Rising 726ft (221 meters) above the canyon floor, **Hoover Dam** ❶ generates electricity for Los Angeles. The lake also

Nevada time clock on the Hoover Dam

supplies water to the cities of Anaheim and San Diego, California – but not Las Vegas. The conspicuous consumption of electrical power and water on the Las Vegas Strip was originally conceived in the belief that the city would have unlimited resources from the dam, but while the populations of both Las Vegas and Southern California grew, no such water or power was available to Las Vegas. Today, the Strip's electricity comes from a coal-fired power plant located to the north of the city, while its water comes from wells, as the municipal government fights with farmers and ranchers in outlying areas for the right to pump more water from the ground.

Hoover Dam Visitors' Center

After paying the admission fee to the **Hoover Dam Visitors' Center**, you can sign up for a tour that takes you into the depths of the dam's interior for a close-up look at the huge generators and spillway. For free, you can walk on the sidewalk along the top of the dam, stare down at the curved expanse of concrete that fills the canyon below, and admire the strangely symbolic Art Deco statues and mosaics. Because of security concerns since the 9/11 terrorist attacks, day packs, large purses, and similar-size bags are not allowed on or inside the dam.

GRAND CANYON WEST

As you drive across Hoover Dam, you are entering the state of Arizona. Notice the clocks on each end of the dam. In the winter months, it is one hour later in Arizona, which is on Mountain Time, than in Nevada, which is on Pacific Time. But since Arizona does not observe Daylight Saving Time, during the summer months the time is the same on both sides of the dam. Continue south for 42 miles (68km) on US Highway 93 to the turnoff on the left marked with a large billboard for **Grand Canyon West** ❷. Follow Pearce Ferry Road for 30 miles (48km) to a well-marked Y-junction, where the right fork – Diamond Bar Road – goes another 15 miles (24km) to Grand Canyon West.

Attractions

Owned by the Hualapai Indian Tribe, whose reservation spans more than 100 miles (160km) of the Grand Canyon Rim, this recreation area will probably have a resort hotel and Indian casino someday. But for now, its attractions include a petting zoo, wagon rides, Indian cultural performances at **Hualapai Ranch**, a hiking trail to a scenic canyon overlook at Guano Point, site of a historic, long-abandoned bat manure mine, and Grand Canyon West's premier attraction, the Skywalk.

The Skywalk

A cantilevered, gulp-inducing glass walkway, the **Skywalk** ❸ protrudes out from the canyon rim in a U-shape

Guano Point

Skywalk

with no visible means of support, letting visitors stare straight down at the Colorado River some 4,000ft (1,219 meters) below. Although it feels frighteningly unsafe, engineering reports assure visitors that the bridge can support more than 71 million lbs (32 million kg), withstand hurricane-force winds, and survive a magnitude 8.0 earthquake. Though the walkway is glass, it is supported by more than 1 million lbs of structural steel. On a first-come, first-served basis, 120 people are allowed on the Skywalk at one time. You cannot just buy a ticket to the Grand Canyon Skywalk, you must buy the Legacy Package ($47 + tax) to enter the Skywalk – or it must be included in the tour you book from Las Vegas.

BACK TO LAS VEGAS

By now it will probably be around 2pm. Retrace your route from Grand Canyon West back over Hoover Dam. From there, you may wish to save time by driving back to the city via US Highway 93/95 instead of Lakeshore Drive. This route will take you back through **Boulder City**, a charming little all-American town built by the federal government to house dam construction workers away from the temptations of Las Vegas. Gambling is not allowed here. The entire return trip along this route should take about two hours, bringing you back to your hotel in plenty of time to rest up for dinner and a show.

MOTEL
Holiday
MOTEL

PALAZZO

nope
DO NOT DISTURB
LINQ

DIRECTORY

Hand-picked hotels and restaurants to suit all budgets and tastes, organised by area, plus select nightlife listings, an alphabetical listing of practical information, and an overview of the best books and films to give you a flavour of the city.

Accommodations	**84**
Restaurants	**94**
Nightlife	**104**
A–Z	**110**
Books and Film	**122**

Master Bedroom at The Mirage

ACCOMMODATIONS

Northern Strip

Circus Circus Hotel, Theme Park, and Casino

2880 Las Vegas Boulevard South; tel: 702-734-0410 or 800-634-3450; www.circuscircus.com; $

The granddaddy of all themed resorts on the Strip, Circus Circus is gaudy fun and a good place for families to stretch their dollar (room specials run as low as $45 per night). Aside from Big Top performers, the Adventuredome, and a carnival, the hotel has a pool and seven restaurants, including one of the largest buffets in Las Vegas. The renovated lobby is classy, but you cannot expect Strip accommodations at this price without compromise: the decor is typical chain-hotel style, with blue carpeting and blonde-wood furniture. Choose from 3,773 rooms and suites in the main hotel (the newest are in the West Tower) and motor lodge, or camp in the 399-site RV Park, the Strip's only campground.

The Mirage

3400 Las Vegas Boulevard South; tel: 702-791-7188 or 800-627-6667; www.mirage.com; $–$$$$

The first of the Strip's post-1950s themed resorts, the Polynesian Mirage is the best resort for nature lovers. Guests can enjoy waterfalls, a lagoon, and Siegfried & Roy's Secret Garden, home to white lions and tigers and a family of Atlantic bottlenose dolphins. Most of the 3,000-plus rooms and suites showcase marble and canopied beds; six have lanais (decks) with a private garden and pool; and eight are exclusive two- and three-bedroom villas. Spread across the resort are two pools, a spa, six fine-dining restaurants, eight casual-dining restaurants, and various bars and lounges.

SLS Las Vegas

2535 Las Vegas Boulevard South; tel: 702-761-7000; www.slslasvegas.com; $–$$$$

This stylish hotel on the Strip is 1.3 miles (2.1km) from the Las Vegas Convention Center and 4 miles (7km) from McCarran International Airport. Stylish rooms and suites offer sitting areas, 55-inch flat-screen TVs and designer toiletries. Some suites have separate living spaces. A resort fee covers in-room Wi-Fi. There are eight dining options, including Japanese and Mediterranean restaurants. Other amenities include a casino, 3 nightclubs and a spa. The resort fee includes access to the rooftop pool and the fitness center. The hotel also has 16 meeting rooms, including a ballroom.

Treasure Island

3300 Las Vegas Boulevard South; tel: 702-894-7111 or 800-944-7444;

Swimming pool at The Venetian

www.treasureisland.com; $$$
A recent renovation has ditched the child-oriented motif in favor of a more grown-up theme. Both affordable and comfortable, the rooms are set within a Y-shaped tower, with the least-expensive rooms on the lower floors and the more expensive ones higher up.

Venetian Resort, Hotel, and Casino

3355 Las Vegas Boulevard South; tel: 702-414-1000 or 877-283-6423; www.venetian.com; $$–$$$$+
A gorgeous rendition of La Bella Italia, the all-suite Venetian is a super-resort aimed at those with very deep pockets. Marble, frescoes, and velvet abound and authentic gondolas ply a series of canals connected to exclusive shops, while street performers entertain in the replica St. Mark's Square. The 4,000 suites in the two 36-story towers average 700 sq ft (65 sq meters) and amenities include king-size canopied beds, sunken living rooms, wet bars, two TVs, high-speed Internet, and personal fax/printer/copier.

Wynn Las Vegas

3131 Las Vegas Boulevard South; tel: 702-770-7000 or 888-320-9966; www.wynnlasvegas.com; $$$$+
Entrepreneur Steve Wynn's eponymous venture is the city's only Mobil and AAA Five-Star resort and reflects the owner's personal touch throughout, from the Wynn signature writ large on the outside to his personal introductions on the hotel's lavish website. Plush rooms offer floor-to-ceiling windows, pillow-top mattresses and tubs, plus Wi-Fi access, iPhone docks, and flat-screen TVs. Luxe suites add individual features like massage rooms, granite wet bars, whirlpool tubs, and/or free in-room breakfast. Amenities include 2 luxe spas, gyms, pools, and hot tubs, as well as an 18-hole golf course. There are four trendy nightclubs and live theater experiences like *Le Rêve* – The Dream, plus 260,000sq ft (24,100sq meters) of meeting space. Dining options range from gourmet restaurants to relaxed cafés.

Southern Strip

Bally's Las Vegas

3645 Las Vegas Boulevard South; tel: 702-967-4111 or 800-634-3434; www.ballyslv.com; $$$
Bally's is one of the oldest hotels on the Strip, but also one of the most overlooked. Large rooms with a modern flair feature overstuffed furniture and subdued earth tones. The hotel has a beautiful pool area, which is perfect for hot days.

Price for a double room for one night with breakfast:
$$$$ = over $300
$$$ = $200–300
$$ = $100–200
$ = below $100

The Bellagio

Bellagio

3600 Las Vegas Boulevard South; tel: 888-987-6667; www.bellagioresort.com; $$$$

Occupying the former site of the Dunes hotel and stealing the scene in the movie *Ocean's Eleven*, the Bellagio is one of the city's most lavish resorts. The beautiful accommodations are split between the main Italianate building and the newer Spa Tower, and even the standard rooms are satisfyingly plush and feature deluxe beds, huge marble bathrooms with tubs and showers big enough for two, and flat-screen TVs. There is an incredible array of fine-dining options, including Lago from the Michelin-decorated chef Julian Serrano. And on top of all that, there's a luxurious spa and a renowned golf course.

Caesars Palace

3570 Las Vegas Boulevard South; tel: 702-731-7110 or 800-634-6661; www.caesarspalace.com; $$–$$$$

This extravagant Las Vegas casino-hotel, a homage to Rome at its most decadent, has been pulling out all the stops since it opened in 1966. There are 2,400 elegant guest rooms and suites with fabulous bathrooms and plenty of amenities, including butler service (at penthouse level), four pools set in extensive gardens, a floating cocktail lounge, 23 restaurants, including those run by celebrity chefs Bradley Ogden and Wolfgang Puck, a world-class spa, three casinos, a nightclub and show venue, and an exclusive high-end shopping arcade.

The Cosmopolitan of Las Vegas

3708 Las Vegas Boulevard South; tel: 702-698-7000; www.cosmopolitanlasvegas.com; $$$$

One of the newest hotels and casino resorts on the Strip is the Cosmopolitan casino hotel, offering views of the adjacent Bellagio fountains. Posh, modern rooms feature floor-to-ceiling windows, flat-screen TVs, Wi-Fi and marble-floored bathrooms; suites add dining areas and kitchenettes with microwaves, stoves, minibars, and wine coolers. Some rooms and suites have balconies. Amenities include an outdoor performance venue, a serene spa and hammam, three pools, a casino, a wedding chapel, a dog-friendly park and several bars and restaurants, including a lobby bar set inside a three-story crystal chandelier.

The Cromwell Las Vegas Hotel & Casino

3595 Las Vegas Boulevard South; tel: 702-777-3777; www.caesars.com/cromwell; $$$$

Guests first entering the Cromwell may feel lost in the dressing room of a Victoria's Secret fashion show. Advertised as a luxury boutique hotel and casino, the abundance of hot pink interlaced with black and white with walnut accents projects the ambiance of a

The entrance to the Cromwell

late-19th-century gentleman's club, a London brothel even. This theme continues throughout the casino floor and even into the sumptuous hotel rooms, with hardwood floors, vintage lamps, headboards, and wallpaper that pay homage to the glamor of Hollywood's golden age. The hotel also features Giada De Laurentiis's first-ever restaurant, which serves up the celebrity chef's lighter, Californian take on Italian classics. And not to be missed – whether you stay at the Cromwell or not – is Drai's, a luxury beach club by day, an erotically charged club by night. The 65,000sq-ft (6,000sq-meter) club features celebrity guests, top DJs, and unparalleled views of Caesars and the Bellagio fountains that will remind you why Vegas is year after year the world's premier party destination.

Delano Las Vegas

3940 Las Vegas Boulevard South; tel: 702-632-7888; www.delanolasvegas.com; $$$$

Something completely new on the Strip, the Delano is a smoke-free, gaming-free resort for the sophisticated traveler. Guests can visit the adjoining Mandalay Bay hotel to try their hands at the tables or slots, but Delano provides a stress- and worry-free environment unheard of in Sin City. And it is a hit. Globetrotters from all over are coming to experience the oasis that was inspired by the Mojave Desert. No matter what room you stay in, you will feel like you've just checked into a spa resort. Every accommodation is considered a suite, complete with one bedroom, master bath, guest bath, and private living area. Even your pets can feel like royalty in the dog-friendly suites available.

Encore

3131 Las Vegas Boulevard South; tel: 702-770-7171; www.wynnlasvegas.com/EncoreResort; $$$$

Encore plays the younger, more sophisticated sister to the Wynn. Though from the outside both look identical, on the inside the Encore, true to its name, simply offers more. From its suites to its casino floor to its dining to its nightlife, few hotels in the world, let alone in Las Vegas, can compete with its Asian-styled, garden-like scenery, its Sinatra restaurant, or its XS nightclub. And with more five-star awards than any resort in the world, it has the ratings to prove it. XS dazzles as the United States' top nightclub for more than five years. Apart from its one-of-a-kind interior, its cutting-edge sound system, and top-of-the-line pyrotechnics, what separates it from every other Vegas venue is its crowd. XS's patrons tend to be more polite, more sophisticated, and less concerned with everyone else – which can be both good and bad. You won't feel lost in a sea of southern California overflow. You will truly feel like someone special.

Entrance to the Four Seasons

Excalibur

3850 Las Vegas Boulevard South; tel: 702-597-7777 or 877-750-5464; www.excalibur.com/en.html; $$

On the south end of the Strip, this Camelot-themed resort is linked to the neighboring New York New York and Tropicana resorts by overhead pedestrian bridges. Straightforward rooms have flat-screen TVs and Wi-Fi; some have granite bathrooms and modern decor. Suites add living rooms, dining areas, and mini fridges. In addition to the casino, amenities include four pools, a spa, a fitness room, and an arcade. There are several restaurants and bars plus live entertainment, including a medieval joust dinner show.

Flamingo Las Vegas

3555 Las Vegas Boulevard South; tel: 702-733-3111 or 800-732-2111; www.flamingolv.com; $$–$$$

Mobster Bugsy Siegel would hardly recognize the hotel he built in 1946, giving the Las Vegas Strip its start. Little has been left intact to hint at the Flamingo's shady past: today, the rooms feature king-size beds and soft earth-tone decor. A full-wall mirror makes each room seem twice as big as it really is.

Four Seasons Hotel

3960 Las Vegas Boulevard South; tel: 702-632-5000 or 877-632-5000; www.fourseasons.com; $$$$

Attached to Mandalay Bay Resort and Casino, this luxe, Art Deco-style hotel features sophisticated rooms and suites feature floor-to-ceiling windows, as well as mountain or Strip views. All come with marble bathrooms, 24-hour room service, minibars and coffeemakers, as well as free Wi-Fi, flat-screen TVs and iPod docks. There's a chic Italian restaurant/bar, plus an upscale steakhouse. An outdoor pool offers private cabanas and a waterside bar. Other amenities include a spa, a fitness center, and a 24/7 business center.

Harrah's

3475 Las Vegas Boulevard South; tel: 800-214-9110; www.harrahs.com; $$

A four-minute walk from Madame Tussauds and across the Strip from Caesars Palace, this Mardi Gras-themed casino hotel is a stop on the Las Vegas monorail. Straightforward, traditional rooms come with Wi-Fi, flat-screen TVs, and marble showers; suites add living and dining rooms, wet bars, and whirlpool tubs. A resort fee is charged. Perks include a bustling casino, live comedy and music performances, and a nightclub and piano bar. There's also a fitness center, spa, salon, and an outdoor pool.

The Linq

3535 Las Vegas Boulevard South; tel: 800-634-6441; www.caesars.com/linq; $$$$

Room at Mandalay Bay

In the middle of the Strip, this modern resort is an eight-minute walk from the Harrah's Las Vegas monorail station and next to the Linq's entertainment/shopping area. Rooms range from basic options with mini fridges (extra charge) to those with an oval-shaped Roman tub; some rooms offer Strip or mountain views. Suites add separate living areas and bathrooms with soaking tubs and dual sinks. A resort fee covers Wi-Fi for one device and fitness center access. Amenities include a casino with celebrity impersonator dealers, several restaurants and bars, a museum/gallery showcasing classic cars, a showroom, and a seasonal outdoor pool.

Luxor

3900 Las Vegas Boulevard South; tel: 702-262-4000 or 800-288-1000; www.luxor.com; $$

This Egypt-themed casino resort on the south end of the Strip is housed in a 30-story pyramid topped with a 315,000-watt light beam. Standard rooms have traditional furnishings, flat-screen TVs, and Wi-Fi. Suites offer soaking tubs and separate sitting rooms; some have wet bars. Pyramid rooms and suites have slanted walls. The varied dining and drinking options include a steak and seafood bar, a Mexican cantina, a pizza joint, and an Irish pub. Additional perks include a casino, fitness center, spa, and salon, plus an outdoor pool and a wedding venue.

Mandalay Bay Resort and Casino

3950 Las Vegas Boulevard South; tel: 702-632-7777 or 877-632-7000; www.mandalaybay.com; $$–$$$$

On the south end of the Strip, this high-end casino hotel is between The Four Seasons and Luxor. Elegant rooms and suites all have 42-inch flat-screen TVs, seating areas, floor-to-ceiling windows, and soaking tubs; upgrades include living areas, wet bars, and/or Bose sound systems. In addition to the casino, amenities include an 11-acre (4.5-hectare) beach/pool complex with a lazy river, a wave pool, and a topless area. There's also a shark aquarium, upscale shopping, live shows, and destination dining.

MGM Grand

3799 Las Vegas Boulevard South; tel: 702-891-7777 or 877-880-0880; www.mgmgrand.com; $$$

Across from the Tropicana, this colossal, emerald-colored casino resort is fronted by a signature 45ft (14-meter) bronze lion. The modern rooms have sleek furnishings, glass-topped desks, and marble bathrooms; suites add living areas and Roman bathtubs. Some wellness-themed rooms feature air purification systems, aromatherapy diffusers, and access to a special lounge. A resort fee includes Wi-Fi and access to a workout room. Perks include four pools, three whirlpools, and a lazy river, live entertainment, a

Pool Cabana at the Monte Carlo

spa and fitness center, a huge casino, trendy nightclubs, and numerous fine-dining and casual restaurants.

Monte Carlo

3770 Las Vegas Boulevard South; tel: 702-730-7777 or 888-529-4828; www.montecarlo.com; $$–$$$

Adjacent to CityCenter on the Strip, this upscale casino resort boasts traditional rooms offer flat-screen TVs, and some upgraded rooms have views of the Strip. Suites add mini fridges, wet bars, and/or whirlpool tubs. The casino has table games, slot machines, and a poker room. There are multiple restaurants, bars, and lounges, as well as renowned entertainment acts. Other amenities include a spa, four pools, and a 400ft (120-meter) lazy river. The resort fee includes access to the fitness center and daily craps table lessons.

Motel 8 Las Vegas

3961 Las Vegas Boulevard South; tel: 702-739-1777; http://motel8lasvegas.yolasite.com; $

This basic roadside motel is across the road from shops and gaming at Mandalay Bay resort and a 14-minute walk from Bali Hai Golf Club. Low-key rooms come with complimentary Wi-Fi and cable TV. Kids aged 18 and under stay free. Amenities include free parking and a seasonal outdoor pool, as well as a convenience store and BBQ facilities.

New York New York

3790 Las Vegas Boulevard South; tel: 702-740-6969 or 866-815-4365; www.nynyhotelcasino.com; $$$

Set between The Monte Carlo and Excalibur, this Big Apple-themed casino hotel on the Strip features several towers built to resemble the New York skyline. Sophisticated rooms have marble bathrooms, Wi-Fi, and flat-screen TVs; suites add whirlpool tubs, mini fridges and Bose stereo systems. Amenities include a rollercoaster 203ft (62 meters) above the Strip, live entertainment, more than a dozen bars and nightclubs, a casino with weekend DJs and go-go dancers, and several restaurants.

The Palazzo

3325 Las Vegas Boulevard South; tel: 702-607-7777; www.palazzo.com; $$$$

Tucked between the Wynn and the Venetian, this upscale, all-suite resort and casino is a six-minute walk from the Fashion Show Mall. Plush accommodations feature Italian-inspired decor and range from modern rooms with flat-screen TVs and soaking tubs to entertainment-focused suites with sunken living rooms, dining areas, and pool tables. The resort fee includes Wi-Fi and fitness center access. Perks include upscale shopping and dining, a modern casino, a Canyon Ranch spa, an outdoor pool, and several chic restaurants and lounges.

Paris Las Vegas

Paris Las Vegas

3655 Las Vegas Boulevard South;
tel: 702-946-7000 or 888-266-5687;
www.parislasvegas.com; $–$$$$

This French-themed casino hotel with a half-size Eiffel Tower is across the Strip from the Bellagio and a nine-minute walk from a Las Vegas monorail station. Most rooms feature traditional, European-inspired decor and have marble bathrooms, flat-screen TVs, and Wi-Fi. Suites add living areas, minibars, and whirlpool tubs. In addition to the casino, amenities include a rooftop pool in a French garden, an indoor Parisian street with live entertainment stages, shopping areas, a lounge with dueling pianos, nightclubs, and several restaurants, including a Gordon Ramsay Steakhouse.

Tropicana Resort and Casino

3801 Las Vegas Boulevard South;
tel: 702-739-2222 or 800-634-4000;
www.tropicanalv.com; $–$$$

Aimed at adult travelers, the Tropicana is one of the few hotels dating back to the "old" Las Vegas of the 1950s and its rates are among the lowest on the Strip. The motif is somewhat Polynesian. The standard rooms are light, plain, and functional, accented by bedspreads and draperies in bright tropical designs. Many on the lower floors look out onto lush foliage that surrounds the pool and offers a buffer against the urban clamor. The tropical pool area has swim-up blackjack tables.

Beyond the Strip

Artisan Hotel

1501 West Sahara Avenue; tel:
702-214-4000 or 800-554-4092;
www.theartisanhotel.com; $$–$$$$

The small Art Deco-style Artisan is located away from the Strip and is the closest thing Las Vegas has to a boutique hotel. Perfect for non-gamblers and business travelers seeking restful surroundings, the Artisan takes its inspiration from European hotels, and incorporates soothing low lighting throughout, as well as original art by Van Gogh, Marc Chagall, and other such celebrated artists. The 64 rooms are all spacious, non-smoking, and include wireless Internet. There is a pool, complimentary daily wine reception at 4.30pm in the lobby, a bar, casual café, and an attractive fine-dining restaurant.

Comfort Inn & Suites

4375 East Craig Road; tel: 702-982-6700;
www.choicehotels.com/nevada/las-vegas;
$

This simple roadside hotel is within walking distance of several restaurants and bus stops (with access to Las Vegas and the Strip), around 1.5 miles (2.5km) from Interstate 15 and 2 miles (3km) from Nellis Air Force Base. All rooms have en-suite bathrooms with showers, as well as free Wi-Fi, flat-screen TVs, microwaves, mini fridges, and coffeemakers. Suites add separate living spaces. Free perks include a hot breakfast buffet and RV parking.

Swimming pool at the Hard Rock

The hotel also offers computers for guest use and meeting space. Other amenities include an outdoor pool, a hot tub, an exercise room, and a convenience store.

Golden Gate Hotel

1 Fremont Street; tel: 702-385-1906 or 800-426-1906; www.goldengatecasino.com; $

This 1906-built, 106-room hotel and casino in Downtown is the oldest and smallest hotel in Vegas – now dwarfed by the Golden Nugget Casino and the Fremont Street Experience. Rooms are standard, with just a few mod-cons.

Hard Rock Hotel and Casino

4455 Paradise Road; tel: 702-693-5000 or 800-473-7625; www.hardrockhotel.com; $–$$$$

Situated behind a branch of the world-famous Hard Rock Cafe, with its original rock'n'roll memorabilia, high-priced hamburgers, and waitresses dressed in 1950s-style uniforms, the Hard Rock Hotel and Casino attracts a celebrity clientele. There are poolside concerts starring today's best musicians, intimate shows in the small concert hall and lounge, a popular see-and-be-seen pool area, a spa and health club, and five restaurants serving everything from comfort food and tacos to Las Vegas's best Japanese food in fashionable Nobu. The 600 ultra-modern rooms and suites have wide-screen plasma TVs and Bose CD systems. Otherwise, the furnishings are so minimal that even the rowdiest of rock bands would have a hard time trashing them.

Hilton Lake Las Vegas Resort and Casino

1610 Lake Las Vegas Parkway, Henderson; tel: 702-567-4700; www3.hilton.com; $$$$

This waterfront resort and spa in desert surroundings 8 miles (13km) off US-95 is 1 mile (0.5km) from Reflection Bay Golf Club and 9 miles (14.5km) from Sam Boyd Stadium. Airy rooms and suites come with 42-inch flat-screen TVs, free Wi-Fi, desks, and mini fridges. There's an outdoor pool, a hot tub, a spa, and a fitness center. Dining is available at a café with an outdoor terrace, a bar and lounge serving light meals, and a poolside bar and grill. There's also a business center, meeting rooms, and garage parking. A resort fee covers Internet access, a shuttle to the Las Vegas Strip, and exercise classes.

Hooters Casino Hotel

115 East Tropicana Avenue; tel: 702-739-9000 or 866-584-6687; www.hooterscasinohotel.com; $$$

Based on the sports bars/restaurants featuring well-endowed Hooters Girls clad in skimpy T-shirts and bikinis, this party-loving hotel offers plenty of fun-in-the-sun activities for the lads. The 650 rooms and suites located in the hotel, tower, or bungalows have a relaxed tropical Florida theme.

Lobby at the Vdara

Motel 6

195 East Tropicana Avenue;
tel: 702-798-0728; www.motel6.com/en;
$$$

Location is everything at this low-rise motel next to Hooters and the Tropicana, within a few blocks' walk of the coolest casino resorts on the Las Vegas Strip. The rooms are as Spartan as you'd expect at a Motel 6, and the desk clerk sits behind steel bars. But, if all you really need is an air-conditioned, no-frills place to change clothes, with a bed, a shower, a phone, and a TV set, this is it. (Note that the motel does have a swimming pool.) Room rates vary dramatically from day to day. During the week, you may pay about the same as a semi-private room at a youth hostel, but on weekends, expect to pay much more.

Palace Station Hotel and Casino

2411 West Sahara Avenue; tel: 702-367 2411; toll free: 1-800-634 3101; www.palacestation.com; $$

Located just off the Strip near Interstate 15, the Palace Station's best rooms are within the tower, built in 1991, while original rooms are in a two-story building surrounding the pool. If possible, request one of the corner rooms, which have larger bathrooms. 1,030 rooms.

Red Rock Casino Resort and Spa

11011 West Charleston; tel: 702-797 7777, toll free: 1-866-767 7773; www.redrocklasvegas.com;
$$

Far from the Strip but convenient for Red Rock Canyon and Mount Charleston, this ultra-elegant spa resort features attractive packages, as well as a host of great restaurants. 818 rooms.

Vdara Hotel and Spa

2600 West Harmon Avenue;
tel: 702-590-2111; www.vdara.com/en.html; $$$$

This 57-story, all-suite, eco-friendly hotel was designed for vacationers looking for a Vegas vacation without so much of the Vegas. The entire property is free from smoke and gambling and is even dog-friendly for those of you who wish not to leave home without your favorite companions. Vdara's rooms borrow from both contemporary and retro styles, and even the most basic of them offer kitchenettes, soaking tubs, and windows with views of the Strip sure to inspire envy in your friends who chose a budget resort. At the other end of the scale, the two-story penthouse with two bedrooms adds every amenity you could possibly desire, including a pull-out sofa bed in the living room, a second bathroom, a washer and dryer, and a private elevator key. Vdara Pool and Lounge comes complete with spa, salon, and fitness center. Drink and eat while you peruse the amazing view.

Buffet at the Bouchon

RESTAURANTS

Northern Strip

AquaKnox

The Venetian, 3355 Las Vegas Boulevard South; tel: 702-414-3772; www.venetian.com; daily 5.30–10pm; $$$$

Celebrity chef Tom Moloney, formerly with the Wolfgang Puck restaurant empire, flies in fresh seafood daily from around the world to prepare dishes such as tuna tataki and wild Tasmanian sea trout. It's all served up in a cool, ocean-hued setting.

Bouchon

The Venetian, 3355 Las Vegas Boulevard; tel: 702-414-6200; www.venetian.com; daily 7am–1pm, until 2pm Fri–Sun, 5–10pm; $$$

Located in the Venezia Tower, Bouchon brings to Las Vegas the top cuisine and service that have made it a Napa Valley institution. Drawn from chef Thomas Keller's memories of traveling through France, Bouchon serves an award-winning menu of bistro classics and daily specials, featuring the best seasonal products available. Enjoy delicious desserts, an extensive selection of raw seafood, a full bar, and superb wine service in the warm and elegant main dining room or amid a beautiful poolside garden setting.

Price guide for an average two-course meal for one with a glass of house wine:
$$$$ = over $60
$$$ = $40–60
$$ = $20–40
$ = under $20

CUT Las Vegas

The Grand Canal Shoppes, 3325 Las Vegas Boulevard South; tel; 702-607-6300; www.wolfgangpuck.com; daily 5.30–11pm; $$$$

From prime dry- and wet-aged beef to shellfish and sautéed and roasted whole fresh fish, CUT provides broad appeal. In addition to the restaurant's renowned signature cuts of beef, guests can enjoy an extensive array of entrées, including the Kobe-style beef short ribs "Indian spiced," slowly cooked for eight hours; sautéed Dover sole à la meunière, with preserved lemon; and whole-roasted Loup de Mer with Moroccan charmoula. A carefully crafted wine list offers an extensive international list of more than 500 selections, focusing mainly on wines from the United States, France, Italy, Spain, and Australia. In addition to an emphasis on robust red wines, the list also features a strong selection of white wines.

Delmonico's Steakhouse

The Venetian, Casino Level, 3355 Las Vegas Boulevard South; tel: 702-414-3737; www.venetian.com; daily 11.30am–2pm and Sun–Thu 5–10pm,

AquaKnox

until 10.30pm Fri–Sat; $$$$

Emeril Lagasse's Delmonico's Steakhouse delivers on hearty, imaginative, creole-infused meat-and-potatoes fare and even richer desserts known and loved by millions because of the celebrity chef's popular TV shows. Among the signature dishes are starters including steak tartare and gumbo, entrées such as pork chops with bacon-wrapped shrimp and bourbon smashed sweet potatoes, and charbroiled dry-aged beef sirloin accompanied by bacon-cheddar twice-baked potato, creole tomato glaze, and horseradish cream. Desserts such as banana bread pudding with ice cream and fudge sauce and whisky crème brûlée are no less impressive. Reservations are necessary. Lagasse also has a creole fish house, Emeril's, in the MGM Grand.

Hash House A Go Go

The Linq 3535 Las Vegas Boulevard South; tel: 702-254-4646; www.hashhouseagogoatlinq–hub.com; daily, 24 hours; $$

If you have the munchies after partying the night away in Las Vegas, then this is the place to go. Hash House A Go Go is home to one of the city's best breakfasts, including oversized flapjacks, breakfast scrambles, signature hashes, farm Benedicts, and more. At lunch and dinner, the Las Vegas casual dining menu features chicken and sage waffles, one-pound burgers stuffed with bacon and mashed potatoes (or other scrumptious delights), sandwiches like the Kokomo (stuffed with meatloaf and smoked mozzarella) and a multitude of salads.

Joe's Seafood Prime Steak and Stone Crab

Forum Shops at Caesars, 3500 Las Vegas Boulevard South; tel: 702-792-9222; www.joes.net; daily 11.30am–10pm, Fri–Sat until 10.30pm; $$$

Fans of this Miami-spawned favorite inside the Forum Shops at Caesars claim it's better than the original thanks to an extensive, diverse menu packed with incredibly fresh seafood, perfectly cooked steaks, and to-die-for desserts. With a professional yet amiable staff providing five-star service in a traditional room that recalls old Vegas, it's a special treat that's well worth the expense.

Palm Restaurant

Forum Shops at Caesars, 3500 Las Vegas Boulevard South; tel: 702-732-7256; www.thepalm.com; daily 11.30am–11pm; $$$

You can't go wrong with this classic New York-born steakhouse in the Forum Shops at Caesars, serving tremendous meats, monstrous lobsters, and decadent desserts in an intimate dining room with cartoon art or on a fun patio ideal for people-watching. An amazing staff that caters to the customer is part of the high-quality package; the more affordable prix-fixe lunch offers some relief.

Diamond and Gold Lasagna at the Portofino

Portofino

The Mirage, 3400 Las Vegas Boulevard South; tel: 866-339-4566; www.mirage.com; Mon, Thu–Sun 5–10pm; $$$

This "*ristorante* and wine lounge," formerly known as Onda Ristorante, has consistently been voted Las Vegas's best Italian restaurant in newspaper surveys. The menu mixes regional and classic Italian dishes with North American innovations, featuring selections such as capellini with scallops, veal marsala, and softshell crabs. From the handmade pasta to the finest imported ingredients to the dozens of fine wines, you'll get a true taste of Italy right on the Strip. Reflecting the quaint, beautiful, and wealthy Italian village it's named after, Portofino is tucked away from all the casino noise, offering large leather booths, beautiful marble, vintage wood fixtures, and Tuscan-style chandeliers. The white linen cloths and rustic Italian decor bring you close to the old world while dim lighting and classical music create an intimate, romantic atmosphere.

SW Steakhouse

Wynn Las Vegas, 3131 Las Vegas Boulevard South; tel: 702-770-3325; www.wynnlasvegas.com; daily 5.30–10pm; $$$$

While you dine on exceptional American steakhouse fare, you'll be dazzled by the nightly shows that happen on the Lake of Dreams, making chef David Walzog's award-winning SW Steakhouse a delight to all the senses. SW Steakhouse is a world-renowned as a purveyor of outstanding quality food.

Top of the World

Stratosphere Tower, 2000 Las Vegas Boulevard South; tel: 702-380-7777; www.topoftheworldlv.com; daily 11am–11pm: $$$$

Located 800ft (244 meters) above the Las Vegas Strip in the Stratosphere Casino, Hotel and Tower, the award-winning Top of the World restaurant offers an unparalleled dining experience. Enjoy breathtaking views of Las Vegas as the restaurant revolves 360 degrees every 80 minutes.

Yardbird Southern Table & Bar

3355 Las Vegas Boulevard South; tel: 702-297-6541; www.runchickenrun.com; daily 11am–midnight, Fri–Sat until 1am; $$

A house of worship to farm-fresh ingredients, classic Southern cooking, culture, and hospitality. Helmed by award-winning restaurateur John Kunkel, this traditional Southern eatery was named among America's best new restaurants in 2012 for its themed decor, chicken and waffles, grits and more, plus craft cocktails.

Yard House

The Linq, 3545 Las Vegas Boulevard South; tel: 702-597-0434; www.yardhouse.com; daily 11am–1am, Fri–Sat until 1.30am; $$

The Linq Promenade is a recent attempt to shift some of the attractions of the Strip outdoors, but the best reason to visit here is a bar called the Yard House. It's actually a chain, with about 100 bars across the whole of the US, but don't let

L'Atelier de Joel Robuchon

that fool you – this is one of the best bars you'll ever visit. It's big inside, but it's tasteful; it's modern, but maintains an elegant look and feel. The food here is excellent and there's a choice of literally hundreds of different craft beers, bitters, and ales on draft. There are TVs, but this isn't a sports bar. Even if you're not a particularly big beer drinker, there's enough choice here to tempt even the most tentative of tasters.

Southern Strip

Andre's

Monte Carlo, 3770 Las Vegas Boulevard South; tel: 702-798-7151; www.andrelv.com; Tue–Sun 5.30–10pm, closed Mon; $$$

If you definitely do not want to eat a stratospherically expensive meal inside a casino resort surrounded by people in shorts and flip flops, this chic French restaurant is for you. Situated in a 1930s Provençal-style home, Andre's was the city's first successful French restaurant and offers an intimate dining experience – like eating a fine meal in an elegant home lovingly cooked by a friend who happens to be a gourmet chef. Try the snails, scallops, mustard-crusted rack of lamb, and braised veal cheek. The sweet dessert soufflés are out of this world, and the wine cellar is extensive. Reservations are essential. Formal attire is suggested.

L'Atelier de Joel Robuchon

MGM Grand, 3799 Las Vegas Boulevard South; tel: 702-891-7358; www.mgmgrand.com; daily 5–10.30pm; $$$$

Very expensive even for a Las Vegas signature restaurant, L'Atelier serves either à la carte, with entrées such as suckling pig confit and sea bass on a bed of baby leeks, or from dégustation and découverte menus that offer arrays of tasting portions. The setting is dramatically hip.

Aureole

Mandalay Bay Resort, 3950 Las Vegas Boulevard South; tel: 702-632-7401; www.aureolelv.com; Mon–Sat 5.30–10.30pm, closed Sun; $$$$

Dinner theater takes on new meaning in Las Vegas's best restaurants, where gourmet food meets out-of-this-world fantasy settings, and it's hard to beat the drama of chef Charlie Palmer's Aureole. Its centerpiece is a glassed-in, 42ft (13-meter) wine tower containing 10,000 bottles of wine, and "the show" consists of watching "wine angels" ascend and find your bottle of wine (ordered via electric sommelier, no less), then descend with your chosen vintage. The food here scales other heights. A lavish, prix-fixe, seven-course meal might include a duet of ahi tuna, three-cheese ravioli accompanied by Dungeness crab, roasted Chilean sea bass, Sonoma squab and seared foie gras, filet mignon and shepherd's pie, and tarte Tatin. Thankfully, an à la carte menu is available for those with both budgets and appetites closer to the ground. Either way, save room for one of the out-of-this-world desserts. Reservations highly recommended. Formal dress.

Meatballs at Carbone

Border Grill

Mandalay Bay Hotel, Beach Level, 3950 Las Vegas Boulevard South; tel: 702-632-7403; www.bordergrill.com; daily 11am–10pm, Fri–Sat until 11pm; $$

With its perfect poolside setting, bright colors, and hip, fun food, Border Grill offers a cuisine inspired by the spices and flavors of Mexico and beyond. US TV chefs Mary Sue Milliken and Susan Feniger personally oversee this branch of their flagship Santa Monica restaurant, so bet on quality and consistency. Try chicken tortilla soup, a selection of tamales, cochinita pibil (a Yucatan pork dish slow-cooked in banana leaves) and pescado Veracruzana (halibut in a garlic and wine broth with tomatoes and olives). The taquería upstairs offers takeout tacos filled with carne asada (sliced, seared steak), beans, cheese, fish, and beef brisket. Standout dining at great prices in an airy atmosphere.

Carbone

3730 Las Vegas Boulevard South; tel: 877-230-2742; www.aria.com; daily 5.30–10.30pm; $$$$

Inspired by red-sauce Italian joints from the 1950s and '60s, the waiters are clad in red velvet tuxedos and the Caesar salads are tossed tableside. The large room is decorated with Rat Pack-era accents and gold-tipped lighting and the other room has big leather banquettes and a dramatic Murano glass chandelier from an old Ferrari showroom.

Charlie Palmer Steakhouse

Four Seasons Hotel, 3960 Las Vegas Boulevard South; tel: 702-632-5120; www.charliepalmer.com; daily 5–10.30pm, closed Sun; $$$$

Celebrity chef Charlie Palmer presents most of his signature dishes here, such as wood-grilled filet mignon and an astonishing 48-oz New York strip steak for die-hard carnivores. Seafood or family-style side dishes are available to non-meat eaters. Premises are spacious, with a clubby atmosphere accented by rich polished wood.

Craftsteak

MGM Grand, 3799 Las Vegas Boulevard South; tel: 702-891-7318; www.craftrestaurant.com; Sun–Thu 5–10pm, Fri–Sat until 10.30pm; $$$$

Using simple ingredients flown in fresh daily from small family farms, award-winning chef Tom Colicchio creates striking presentations of flavorful dishes, including lobster, wild king salmon, and the house specialty, grilled Kobe skirt steak. There is also an extensive wine list.

Crush

MGM Grand, 3799 Las Vegas Boulevard South; tel: 702-891-3222; www.crushmgm.com; Sun–Thu 5.30–10.30pm, Fri–Sat 5–11.30pm; $$$$

Crush pays homage to the age of communal feasting, where dinner out is more than sustenance – it's a party. It serves a cosmopolitan shared-plates menu by chef Billy DeMarco, with small

The patio at the Picasso

plates and not-so-small plates for sharing and pairing. The menu includes a range of offerings to satisfy both the foodie and casual diner, from tender octopus and jalapeno ceviche, to sliced steak with crushed potatoes.

Eiffel Tower Restaurant

Paris Hotel, 3655 Las Vegas Boulevard South; tel: 702-948-6937; www.eiffeltowerrestaurant.com; daily 4.30–10.30pm, Fri–Sat until 11pm; $$$$

Chef J. Joho's gourmet Gallic entrées are served in an elegant, contemporary atmosphere. Expect dishes such as blue cheese soufflé pudding, tournedos Rossini with foie gras and truffle sauce, and a spectacular seafood platter.

Fix

Bellagio, 3600 Las Vegas Boulevard South; tel: 702-693-8865; www.bellagio.com; Sun–Thu 5–11pm, Fri–Sat until midnight; $$$$

This huge, architecturally impressive space is a combined bar, club, and restaurant serving elegant American comfort food. The menu includes tomato soup, mushroom bisque, crab cakes, sashimi, caviar, roast chicken, Kobe beef, rib-eye steak, milk shakes, and root-beer floats. A good place for a martini or mojito and a bite to eat while watching the casino action.

Javier's

The Shops at Crystals, 3730 Las Vegas Boulevard South; tel: 866-590-3637; www.javiers-cantina.com; daily 5.30–10.30pm, Fri–Sat until 11.30pm; $$$

A feat of culinary delights awaits here, including hand-shaken margaritas, ceviche, enchiladas, and steak, not to mention a selection of the world's finest tequilas. You'll find all the makings for a memorable Mexican meal at Javier's, with unique architectural elements like a spectacularly detailed chainsaw wood carving with an Aztec motif.

Michael Mina

Bellagio, 3600 Las Vegas Boulevard South; tel: 702-693-7223; www.michaelmina.net; daily 5.30–10pm, closed Wed; $$$$

An impressive dining experience awaits at this Bellagio offshoot of Michael Mina's San Francisco New American, where an expertly prepared menu with exquisite seafood offerings is presented by servers who will enthusiastically discuss what's special about every dish. This is a beautiful setting in an oasis of calm amid the hustle and bustle of the Strip, making the considerable expense of your evening worth every cent.

Picasso

Bellagio, 3600 Las Vegas Boulevard South; tel: 702-693-8865; www.bellagio.com; Wed–Mon 5.30–9.30pm, closed Tue; $$$$

Who wouldn't want to enjoy a sumptuous meal surrounded by original Picassos? Inside chef Julian Serrano's latest French restaurant at the Bellagio, the unsurpassed setting complements the astonishing art collection with spectacular views of the fountains; meanwhile, a

Prime Steakhouse

top-notch staff serves prix-fixe dinners as opulent and rich as the locale. Granted, this masterpiece commands a master price, but it's earned for delivering the meal of your dreams.

Prime Steakhouse

Bellagio, 3600 Las Vegas Boulevard South; tel: 702-693-8865; www.bellagio.com; daily 5–10pm; $$$

Dark wood paneling and dining booths secluded by ornate tapestry curtains create a romantic setting in which to savor master chef Jean-Georges Vongerichten's works of culinary art. Though it styles itself as a steakhouse, the restaurant's menu features only a couple of beef dishes among more creative offerings such as seared tuna au poivre with wasabi-mashed potato and steamed bok choy.

Spago

Forum Shops at Caesars Palace, 3500 Las Vegas Boulevard South; tel: 702-369-6300; www.wolfgangpuck.com; Sun–Thu 11.30am–11pm, Fri–Sat until midnight; $$–$$$

Visionary pizza meister Wolfgang Puck began Las Vegas's gourmet dining in 1992, and he's still at the forefront of fine dining in the city, with no fewer than four restaurants, two of which – Spago and Chinois – are found in Caesars Palace. Spago is a multistory, art-filled, fine-dining restaurant fronted by a casual, less-expensive eatery with sidewalk dining (also at lunchtime) and good casino watching. Smoked salmon pizza remains Puck's signature dish, as well as comfort foods such as pancetta-bacon-wrapped meatloaf and mashed potatoes. In season, yellow-fin tuna, crab cakes, short ribs, and snapper head up the dinner choices. Puck attempts to use organic meats, eggs, dairy, and produce whenever available. Desserts are rich and decadent. Reservations are strongly recommended.

Wicked Spoon Buffet

The Cosmopolitan, 3708 Las Vegas Boulevard South; tel: 702-698-7000; www.cosmopolitanlasvegas.com; Mon–Thu 8am–2pm, 5–9pm, Fri–Sun 8am–3pm, 3–10pm, until 9pm Sun; $$$

A bustling food hall, the Wicked Spoon delivers well-crafted original selections for every appetite. With its mix of top-quality, familiar staples and imaginative seasonal dishes, this Las Vegas eatery satisfies cravings and invites discovery.

Beyond the Strip

Andiron Steak & Sea

1720 Festival Plaza Drive; tel: 702-685-8002; www.andironsteak.com; Mon–Sat 5–10pm, Sun 10am–2pm, 5–10pm; $$$$

This upscale eatery for steaks and seafood, in an elegant white space, is the creation of restauranteur Elizabeth Blau and chef Kim Canteenwalla. It serves up a creative American menu in a beautiful setting that conjures up the best of the upper-class, East Coast settlement of the Hamptons. A must for all serious fans of food.

Carson Kitchen

124 South 6th Street; tel: 702-473-9523;

Heart Attack Grill

www.carsonkitchen.com; daily 11am–10pm, Fri–Sat until 11pm; $$
Inventive but affordable, this funky American kitchen inside the former John E. Carson Hotel, Downtown, serves modern comfort food with a twist, from a fantastic menu full of unexpected combinations, including the not-to-be-missed bacon jam. Supported by a cool rooftop patio and hip, personable servers, this stylish space also offers some innovative cocktails.

Chengdu Taste

3950 Schiff Drive; tel: 702-437-7888; daily 11am–3pm, 5–10pm; $$
Spice specialist Tony Xu brought his wildly popular Sichuan restaurant to Chinatown and it's as packed as any of his locations around the LA-adjacent San Gabriel Valley. This is not a complicated restaurant because the fiery dishes are really the stars of the show here, no embellishments needed. This is a hard-to-find spot near Spring Mountain Road, the Chinatown of Las Vegas. Take a cab to get there – you won't regret it.

Chow

1020 Fremont Street; tel: 702-998-0574; www.chowdtlv.com; Tue–Sat noon–8pm, closed Sun–Mon; $$
Helmed by chef Natalie Young, Chow offers a creative menu with items you never knew you wanted, but now suddenly must have. Start with the Southern-style chicken and rice soup, then move on to an Italian-inspired noodle dish, and end it all with the Fuji apple fritter topped with plum wine caramel sauce.

Eat

707 Carson Avenue; tel: 702-534-1515; www.eatdtlv.com; daily 8am–2pm, until 3pm Mon–Fri; $$
The second offering from chef Natalie Young serves up some serious breakfast eats to delight the masses. Diners can nosh on cinnamon biscuits topped with a smattering of warm strawberry compote, golden pancakes, huevos motulenos (a breakfast made from eggs, tortilla, beans and cheese), chicken fried steak, and much more.

Golden Steer Steakhouse

308 West Sahara Avenue; tel: 702-384-4470; www.goldensteerlasvegas.com; daily 4.30–10.30pm; $$$
For nearly half a century, the Golden Steer has been serving seafood and tasty steaks to locals and visitors in the know, including Vegas legends Frank Sinatra and his Rat Pack, Elvis Presley, and John Wayne. There are historic photographs on the walls, and the waiters wear snappy tuxedos.

Heart Attack Grill

450 Fremont Street; tel: 702-333-5555; www.heartattackgrill.com; daily 11am–10pm; $$
Diners don hospital gowns before indulging in heart attack-inducing fare such as the bypass burger. This is a place where the burgers are bigger than your arm, fries are cooked in lard, and if you're

Michael's Gourmet Room

350+ lbs you eat for free. The Heart Attack Grill nurses/waitresses will prescribe 9,000-calorie burgers, but if you don't take your medicine, be ready for the consequences... as you'll be taken from your table and spanked in front of everyone. Oh yes.

Hugo's Cellar

202 Fremont Street; tel: 702-385-4011; www.hugoscellar.com; daily 5–10pm; $$$

Divine Continental plates and old-school ambiance provide a taste of Las Vegas as it used to be at this romantic Downtown den at the Four Queens casino where every lady receives a rose; the classy package has high-end prices to match, but incomparable service helps make it a favorite among locals, particularly for a special occasion.

Lawry's The Prime Rib

4043 Howard Hughes Parkway; tel: 702-893-2223; www.lawrysonline.com; daily 11.30am–2pm, 5–10pm, Sun 4–9pm; $$$

This throwback Eastside steakhouse captivates carnivores with generous portions of buttery prime rib hand-sliced at the table. Granted, you'll open your wallet wide for the experience, but the Art Deco setting is pretty fabulous and so is the top-notch service.

Lotus of Siam

953 East Sahara Avenue; tel: 702-735-3033; www/lotusofsiamlv.com; Mon–Fri 11am–2.30pm and 5.30–10pm, Sat–Sun 5.30–10pm; $$

Justin Gold of Gourmet magazine has called this the "single best Thai restaurant in North America." The lengthy menu includes not only well-known dishes such as coconut curries, but also the little-known cuisine of northeastern Thailand such as kang-ka-noon (spicy young jackfruit curry), with a choice of pork, chicken, or smoked fish flakes.

Michael's Gourmet Room

9777 Las Vegas Boulevard South; tel: 702-796-7111; www.southpointcasino.com; daily 5.30–10pm; $$$$

Old-school elegance is alive and well at this lovely, but quite pricey, Continental eatery, where the outstanding black-tie service makes you feel like you're a long-lost friend; the magnificent dishes, many of which are prepared tableside, are matched by upscale, Victorian-style surroundings.

Nora's Italian Cuisine

6020 West Flamingo Road; tel: 702-873-8990; www.norascuisine.com; Mon–Thu 11am–10pm, Fri–Sat 11am–midnight, Sun 4–10pm; $$

Delicious meats, pastas, and sauces that captivate your senses await inside this family-run local favorite tucked away on the West Side, where home-style Italian fare shines among awesome cocktails and a nice wine selection; the intimate location can be crowded – regulars say make a reservation – but factor in the reasonable prices and it's well worth the wait.

Pizza Rock Las Vegas

Pamplemousse

400 East Sahara Avenue; tel: 702-733-2066; www.pamplemousserestaurant.com; daily 5–10pm; $$$$

One of Las Vegas's most romantic restaurants for more than 30 years, Pamplemousse combines the ambience of a French country inn with dishes largely inspired by French cuisine, such as onion soup, mussels, and veal medallions with mustard sauce. You can select from the regular menu (not printed, only recited tableside by the waiter), an "epicurean" five-course prix-fixe dinner, or a "gourmet" menu shared by a minimum of 10 guests.

Pizza Rock

201 North 3rd Street; tel: 702-385-0838; www.pizzarocklasvegas.com; Mon–Thu 11am–midnight, Fri–Sat 11am–2am, Sun 10.30am–midnight; $$

Tony Gemignani fronts these lively hangouts providing delicious, inspired pizzas with numerous topping possibilities, plus a tremendous beer list and, oddly enough, very popular burgers. Each of the three burgers on the menu is made with Kobe beef and topped with fresh ingredients in combinations you probably haven't seen before. The Burrata Burger is topped with Burrata cheese, bacon, caramelized onions, arugula (rocket) and a balsamic reduction. The flavors are reminiscent of a traditional bacon cheeseburger but the combination of ingredients brings the burger to a different level.

Raku

5030 West Spring Mountain Road; tel: 702-367-3511; www.raku-grill.com; Mon–Sat 6pm–3am, closed Sun; $$

This cozy West Side grill instills its exquisite, high-end, small offerings with bold, complex flavors and elevates them to another level; solid service and late hours are added benefits, so it's a destination for foodies as well as chefs on their off-hours.

Roy's Las Vegas

620 East Flamingo Road; tel: 702-691-2053; www.roysrestaurant.com; daily 5–10pm, Fri–Sat until 11pm; $$$

Another superb reincarnation of a famed restaurant – this time Roy's Honolulu, the elegant Asian Fusion seafood eatery on the Hawaiian island of Oahu. Among the signature dishes are blackened ahi tuna, hibachi-grilled salmon in ponzu sauce, and Szechuan-spiced baby back pork ribs.

Therapy

518 East Fremont Street; tel: 702-912-1622; www.therapylv.com; Sun–Thu 11.30am–11pm, Fri–Sat until midnight; $$

Downtown Las Vegas's dining scene just keeps getting better and Therapy is one of the very best. A fun spot for lunching professionals and date-night shenanigans, winning dishes like the fried pig ears and red velvet chicken 'n' waffles have cemented themselves as a staple in dining north of Charleston.

Rod Stewart at the Colosseum

NIGHTLIFE

The nightlife in Vegas changes constantly, with big names swapping venues all the time. However, there is always something good on – in fact, the hardest decision you'll probably have to make is which one to go and see; there is always more than enough to choose from. This is a guide to some of the best venues that consistently have good talent on offer. Be sure to always check local listings and the websites for every venue before you decide where you want to go, not least because it's not uncommon to find a hidden gem, or maybe even a band or comedy act that isn't considered A-list, but happens to be a big favorite of yours.

Live music

Bar at Times Square

New York New York, 3790 Las Vegas Boulevard South; tel: 702-740-6466; www.newyorknewyork.com

Located in the heart of New York New York Hotel & Casino, great drinks and dueling pianos are the focus nightly at this boisterous bar. Those who visit during the daytime can watch their favorite sports on one of 14 flat-screen TVs, play bar-top games, and take advantage of the four-hour-long Happy Hour Monday to Friday, featuring Heineken drafts, house wine, and select shooters for just $5 from 3 to 7pm.

Boulevard Pool

The Cosmopolitan, 3708 Las Vegas Boulevard South; tel: 702-698-7778; www.cosmopolitanlasvegas.com

One of Las Vegas' most unique concert venues, the Boulevard Pool is a multi-level pool experience by day and an intimate outdoor concert venue with unobstructed sightlines of both the stage and the Strip by night. Able to accommodate more than 3,000 guests, the seasonal venue is where the resort hosts 90 percent of its shows, as concerts are booked well into October. Most shows are for all ages.

The Colosseum

Caesars Palace, 3570 Las Vegas Boulevard South; tel: 888-929-7849; www.thecolosseum.com

Las Vegas' premier music venue, the Colosseum at Caesars Palace has been home to some of the world's greatest entertainers since opening its doors in 2003. Built at a cost of $95 million, it was originally created for Celine Dion's "A New Day..." but has gone on to host more than 2,000 events. It's also home to one of the largest indoor, high-definition LED screens in the world, standing 110ft (34 meters) wide by 34ft (10 meters) tall and weighing 31 tons.

House of Blues

Mandalay Bay Resort and Casino, 3950 Las

The Colosseum

Mandalay Bay Beach Concert

Vegas Boulevard South; tel: 702-632-7600; www.houseofblues.com

Featuring state-of-the-art sound and lighting technology in a one-of-a-kind custom-designed environment aimed at bringing fans and artists together, the House of Blues inside Mandalay Bay is one of the country's preeminent live music venues – not to mention the Vegas home of Carlos Santana. True to its Southern theme, the House of Blues' decor feels like you've stepped into a Vegas version of New Orleans.

The Joint

Hard Rock Hotel, 4455 Paradise Road; tel: 702-693-5000; www.hardrockhotel.com

Many of the biggest names in music have played The Joint in Hard Rock since it first opened in 1995, including The Rolling Stones, Bob Dylan, Coldplay, The Killers, and more. The Joint doubled its space in 2009, now accommodating 4,000 people in a three-level venue that includes 700 fixed balcony seats, general-admission standing room on the floor, and a second level VIP area with luxury boxes.

Mandalay Bay Beach

Mandalay Bay hotel; 3950 Las Vegas Boulevard South; tel: 702-632-7777; www.mandalaybay.com

One of the Strip's most unique concert-going experiences, Mandalay Bay Beach hosts its summer Beach Concert Series every year from May until September. Music lovers are invited to bring their blankets and sit on the beach or wade in the surf as they listen to some of the biggest names in music perform on a one-of-a-kind stage suspended above the resort's 1.6-million-gallon (7-million-liter) wave pool.

MGM Grand Garden Arena

3799 Las Vegas Boulevard South; tel: 702-531-3826; www.mgmgrand.com

When Barbra Streisand is the first person to perform on your stage, you know you're destined for greatness. Home to major awards shows and music festivals, including the Billboards Music Awards, the Academy of Country Music Awards, and the iHeartRadio Music Festival, the MGM Grand Garden Arena is one of the Strip's top music venues. The multi-purpose venue has hosted numerous world-class concerts over the years, including U2, Madonna, Tina Turner, Bruce Springsteen, and Justin Timberlake.

Napoleon's Lounge

Caesars Palace, 3570 Las Vegas Boulevard South; tel: 702-946-7000; www.caesars.com

Home to resident artist Taylor Hicks, this intimate Parisian lounge is known almost as much for its entertainment line-up as its drinks. In addition to the *American Idol* winner, who performs on select nights, it hosts one of the top dueling pianos shows in town. Guests are encouraged to sing along and join in on the fun as the pianists

Hakkasan

perform a wide variety of hits throughout the evening, many at the audience's request. There's no cover charge for the dueling pianos show, so guests can enjoy even more selections from Napoleon Lounge's drinks menu.

Petrossian Bar

Bellagio, 3600 Las Vegas Boulevard South; tel: 702-693-7111; www.bellagio.com

For a more laid-back evening, head on over to the Bellagio's Petrossian Bar, where guests can enjoy live music from a Steinway grand. Pianists perform daily from 10am to 12.45am and include a range of talented performers, such as David Osborne, who has performed at various White House functions for Presidents Barack Obama, Bill Clinton, and Ronald Reagan. While you're enjoying the music, treat your palate to a house-made infused cocktail or afternoon tea. Petrossian is also known for its selection of fine caviars, making it the perfect place for those with discerning taste.

Toby Keith's I Love This Bar & Grill

Harrah's Las Vegas Casino and Hotel, 3475 Las Vegas Boulevard South; tel: 702-369-5000; http://tobykeithsbar.com

Named for his song "I Love This Bar," Toby Keith's Las Vegas restaurant combines down-home Southern favorites and live country music to make for an experience that's sure to put a big smile on your face. Many of the country acts that perform on the restaurant's stage nightly were hand-picked by Keith himself, so guests know they're in for a real treat. Country music fans can also enjoy the acts without having to pay a cover, giving them another reason to two-step on over.

Nightclubs

1OAK

3400 Las Vegas Boulevard South; tel: 702-693-8300; http://1oaklasvegas.com

This 16,000sq-ft (1,500sq-meter) avant-garde mega-club features Roy Nachum artwork, a state-of-the-art Avalon sound system, a 250-person VIP area, two unique rooms with dedicated DJs, and an enormous stage. Converging art and fashion, famous and infamous, cutting edge and established, barriers have been deliberately torn down to create a sexy and unpredictable environment.

Beacher's Madhouse

MGM Grand, 3799 Las Vegas Boulevard South; tel: 323-785-3036; www.beachersmadhouse.com

Celebrity impersonators are scattered throughout the crowd at this MGM Grand night spot, which rocks a variety show on stage that includes wrestling and heavy metal balancing acts, and even acrobats who deliver bottle service.

Chateau

Paris Las Vegas, 3655 Las Vegas Boulevard South; tel: 702-994-5198; http://chateaunights.com

Chateau gives you the option to dance

Light Nightclub, at the Mandalay Bay

the night away in their club, or take the party outdoors to their second-story terrace or Versailles-style gardens overlooking the Strip. Take in those panoramic views in your VIP cabana, oui?

Hakkasan

MGM Grand, 3799 Las Vegas Boulevard South; tel: 702-891-3838; http://hakkasanlv.com

If you like world-famous DJs (Tiesto, Steve Aoki, Calvin Harris), eating exquisite Chinese food, and imbibing specialty cocktails, odds are you'll seriously enjoy Hakkasan Las Vegas, where having an extra $500,000 lying around buys you their insane Dynastic bottle service package. Don't have that? No worries, $12,000 will still get you the ZEN package with a casual 10 bottles of Dom, two magnums of Grey Goose, and a bottle of Patron Platinum.

Hyde Bellagio

Bellagio, 3600 Las Vegas Boulevard South; tel: 702-693-8700; http://sbe.com/nightlife/locations/hyde-bellagio

They call themselves "the best nightclub in Las Vegas." Get a load of their terrace overlooking the iconic Bellagio fountains, or choose from multiple bottle service packages served by scantily clad ladies in leather. This 10,000sq-footer (900sq meters) is legendary in Vegas for good reason.

Light

Mandalay Bay, 3950 Las Vegas Boulevard South; tel: 702-693-8300; http://thelightvegas.com

Inspired by the same man who brought you Cirque du Soleil, you can expect the same kind of creative, experimental innovation in the performances that come to Light. Smoke and mirrors and people hanging from ropes are just the beginning as old favorites like Skrillex and more bring new ideas to this laboratory of Vegas nightlife.

Marquee

The Cosmopolitan, 3708 Las Vegas Boulevard South; tel: 702-333-9000; www.cosmopolitanlasvegas.com

The Marquee Dayclub is the intersection of fun and luxury. With infinity pools, eight cabanas, and 10 three-story bungalow lofts, this outdoor space is sure to please on a scorching Vegas afternoon. When the sun goes down, the party starts.

Surrender

Wynn Encore, 3121 Las Vegas Boulevard South; tel: 702-770-7300; http://surrendernightclub.com

Surrender at the Wynn Resort boasts a 5,000sq-ft (460sq-meter) dance floor and guest DJ appearances from folks like Diplo and Will.I.Am. So check your "baggy clothes" and "athletic footwear" at the door and dress to impress at this swanky after-hours club.

TAO

The Venetian, 3355 Las Vegas

XS Nightclub

Boulevard South; tel: 702-388-8588; http://taolasvegas.com
This Asian bistro/nightclub/beach club nestled into The Venetian is a staple of Vegas nightlife, offering cutting-edge cuisine and a rotating line-up of DJs and performers.

Tryst

The Wynn, 3131 Las Vegas Boulevard South; tel: 702-770-7000; www.wynnlasvegas.com
This Wynn nightclub, with a subtle, intimate atmosphere as well as an outdoor deck and pool area, boasts a waterfall by the pool and a little bit of breathing room compared to other Vegas late-night staples.

XS

Wynn Encore, 3121 Las Vegas Boulevard South; tel: 702-770-7000; http://xslasvegas.com
Palm trees, pools, and parties in a gold-plated, mirrored, plush interior like you've never seen await you at Wynn's premiere nightclub, XS. The guest list of DJs and performers always keeps it fresh, from Redfoot to Martin Solveig.

Comedy clubs

Brad Garrett's Comedy Club

MGM Grand, 3799 Las Vegas Boulevard South; tel: 866-799-7711; www.bradgarrettcomedy.com
Welcome to the only place in Las Vegas to catch Brad Garrett performing live along with some of the hottest names in stand-up – from established stars to the funniest up-and-comers. To add to the fun factor, every show takes place in a specially designed theater custom-built for comedy.

Four Queens LA Comedy Club

Four Queens Hotel and Casino, 202 East Fremont Street; tel: 702-385-4011; www.thelacomedyclub.com
Great comedy in downtown Vegas! at the Four Queens LA Comedy Club you can check out some of best and brightest comics. Show times are 9pm Tue–Sun, with new local comics appearing eachand every week.

Gordie Brown

Golden Nugget, 129 East Fremont Street; tel: 702-385-7111; www.goldennugget.com
Impressionist, singer and entertainer Gordie Brown is well known for his amazing comedy and celebrity impressions such as Arnold Schwarzenegger, Jack Nicholson, and Sylvester Stallone, as well as Las Vegas icons like Elvis Presley and Sammy Davis, Jr.

LA Comedy Club

2000 Las Vegas Boulevard South; tel: 702-275-1823; www.thelacomedyclub.com
Top comedic talent features in Bally's Windows Theatre, overlooking the Strip.

Brad Garrett's Comedy Club

Las Vegas Live Comedy Club

3667 Las Vegas Boulevard South; tel: 702-260-7200; www.lasvegaslivecomedyclub.com

Bringing together a cross section of the best comedians from NY, Chicago, Boston, LA, and Las Vegas, it's conveniently located inside Miracle Mile Shops inside Planet Hollywood hotel and casino in the center of the Las Vegas Strip.

Las Vegas Zombie Burlesque

3663 Las Vegas Boulevard South; tel: 866-932-71818; www.zombieburlesqueshow.com

Strictly speaking, the Las Vegas Zombie Burlesque Show is not a comedy club, but laughs are guaranteed at this unique show. Describing itself as a "dead sexy comedy musical", the show will take you back to the year 1958: the world has all but been overrun by zombies; heroically, however, the President of the United States has managed to broker a deal with the zombies that allows the two groups to live together in harmony. As part of the deal, the zombies demanded the living hand over their worst criminals, and they duly obliged. As a gesture of appreciation for their co-operation, the zombies want to show the living that they are not all bad. What better way to do so than to open the doors of one of your biggest clubs to your new friends?! The fictional Club Z is now open for business! Expect plenty of laughs.

Laugh Factory

Tropicana, 3801 Las Vegas Boulevard South; tel: 702-739-2222; www.laughfactory.com

This Vegas version of LA's iconic world-famous comedy club adds to the New Tropicana's first-class entertainment, which already boasts A-list performers as well as the newest, local rising stars of stand-up. The Vegas club lets funny run loose, with acts encouraging patrons to "laugh their rears off" on a nightly basis. The small venue is very intimate and as a result, the acoustics are excellent. Although technically a family friendly venue, many of the acts are most certainly not suitable for minors, check the schedule online first if going as a family.

Sin City Comedy Show

Planet Hollywood Resort & Casino, 3667 Las Vegas Boulevard South; tel: 702-777-7776; www.caesars.com

Created by Emmy award-winning writer and comedian John Padon, Sin City Comedy & Burlesque features well-known comedians that you'll recognize from Comedy Central, VH1, HBO or The Late Show with David Letterman. The comics are joined on stage by burlesque dancers: it is rare that a show does both well, but Sin City Comedy & Burlesque certainly does. The all-singing, all-dancing troop of burlesque dancers help to give this joint an authentic, Vegas atmosphere.

The Cleveland Clinic

A–Z

A

Age restrictions

No one under 21 is permitted in casinos, and minors under 18 years of age are not permitted on the Strip without a parent or guardian after 9pm on weekends and holidays. The state of Nevada does not permit anyone under the age of 21 to drink alcohol in public places, and you should keep some kind of picture identification, such as a passport or driving license, on your person, in case you are asked for proof of age.

B

Budgeting

Credit and direct debit cards are accepted throughout Las Vegas. You'll find cash machines in most hotel lobbies. To avoid high surcharges levied on non-bank ATM machine transactions, consider getting cash back from purchases at a non-casino business. The days of rock-bottom deals in Las Vegas may be a thing of the past, but it's still possible to enjoy all-you-can-eat buffets, cheap (or even free) casino bar drinks, and midweek hotel package deals. Today, though, the sheer quality of the lodging and dining options, shows, and attractions is so tempting, a couple should consider budgeting at least $100 per day, excluding accommodations, to take advantage of all Las Vegas has to offer – more if high-end dining and the most popular shows interest you. Big conventions (a year-round phenomenon in Las Vegas) affect prices and cause hotel rooms and shows to sell out. Savvy travelers plan their trips around these, if possible.

C

Children

Child-friendly resorts, such as Circus Circus and Excalibur, often allow kids under 12 to stay for free in their parents' rooms, and have well-priced buffets that are ideal for families. Most hotels have pools, and many provide programs for children and teenagers, while babysitters and childcare facilities are also sometimes available.

Although Las Vegas remains primarily a gaming destination, families will have no difficulty finding activities suited to children on the Strip. In addition to the suggestions on our Las Vegas With Kids tour (see page 48), there's bowling at Orleans and Green Valley Ranch; and a number of outdoor attractions, such as Valley of Fire State Park, Red Rock Canyon, Hoover Dam, and surrounding national parks that

Hallway at the Wynn

are tailor-made for youngsters. A car is recommended if you are visiting with children: walking distances are much greater than they appear, especially in hot desert sun.

Childcare

There are onsite childcare centers at all Coast Casinos and Station Casinos, including the Orleans, Green Valley Ranch, South Coast, Sunset Station, Gold Coast, and Palace Station. Kids aged between 2 and 12 are welcome for a maximum of five hours daily from 9am to midnight (to 1am on Sat). The fee is around $6 per child per hour. Parents must remain on the premises.

The Westin Lake Las Vegas Resort & Spa is an ideal location to take your children and it offers a number of recreational facilities, even if it doesn't make them immediately apparent on its website. To this end, it's probably only advisable to stay here if you do have kids, because the pool can be overrun with children during the day.

Climate

Las Vegas is in the Mojave Desert and is hot and arid with extreme temperature ranges. The average rainfall is just over 4 inches (10.5cm) a year, and humidity is frequently below 10 per cent in summer. Average highs in summer top 100°F (38°C) daily with nighttime lows of 71–81°F (22–27°C). Things start cooling down in November, with winter highs in the upper 60s°F (20°C) and lows in the upper 30s°F (4°C), with higher precipitation and the occasional snowfall. The best time to visit is fall or spring, when daytime temperatures are balmy and nights are cool.

Clothing

In summer, pack light, casual, breathable clothing; a bathing suit; a broad-brimmed hat; sunglasses; neck protection; sunscreen with an SPF of 30 or above; and sturdy lightweight walking sandals or lace-ups for walking the long distances around hotels/casinos and museums, the Strip, Downtown, and excursions to surrounding outdoor attractions. Although shorts and T-shirts are the norm, those in the know bring long-sleeved shirts and pants (trousers) to protect exposed skin from strong sun in summer and fierce air-conditioning inside buildings. Formal attire is rarely necessary: one dress-up outfit for women and a jacket for men are all you'll probably need. Between November and April, temperatures can get surprisingly chilly, so bring a sweater with you. Any time except summer wear layers and carry a waterproof jacket and a hat.

Crime and safety

Visiting Las Vegas is safer than ever these days, with few violent crimes reported and very visible policing, private security guards, and surveillance cameras in public places, as well as

New York New York

VIVA Patrol volunteers trained by the police available to help out in tourist areas. Theft of personal property is quite common, however, so keep an eye on your belongings in busy areas, keep valuables locked in in-room safes, and buckets of coins in your lap, not next to slot machines in casinos.

Currency and taxes

American dollars come in bills of $1, $5, $10, $20, $50, and $100. The dollar is divided into 100 cents. Coins come in 1 cent (penny), 5 cents (nickel), 10 cents (dime), 25 cents (quarter), 50 cents (half-dollar), and $1 denominations.

There is no value-added tax (VAT) in the US, and Nevada does not charge state taxes. The city of Las Vegas does charge a local sales tax, however: 8.1 percent on purchases and 10 percent on hotel rooms (an extra 3 percent tax is added to some rooms on or near the Fremont Street Experience). Car-rental companies charge both sales tax and service fees.

Customs

You can bring the following duty-free items into the US: 1 liter of alcohol (if over 21 years of age); 200 cigarettes, 50 cigars (not Cuban), or 4.4lb (2kg) of tobacco (if over 18 years of age); and gifts worth up to $100 ($800 for US citizens). Travelers with more than $10,000 in US or foreign currency, traveler's checks, or money orders must declare these upon entry. Meats, fruits, vegetables, seeds, or plants (and many prepared foods from them) are not permitted and must be disposed of in the bins provided before entering. For more information, contact US Customs & Border Protection (877-227-5511; www.cbp.gov).

Disabled travelers

Las Vegas attracts many seniors and has the largest number of ADA-accessible guest rooms in the nation. Casinos are almost always on the ground floor, and hotel resorts typically have elevators and ramps in addition to stairs, making them easy to get around for visitors with reduced mobility. For more information, request the free Access Las Vegas brochure from the Las Vegas Convention and Visitors Authority's ADA Coordinator (tel: 702-892-0711; 800-326-8888; www.lasvegas24hours.com).

Electricity

The US uses 110 to 120 volts AC (60 cycles). If visiting from outside North America, you may require an electrical adapter for any electronics or appliances you want to bring. Las Vegas electrical outlets accept the standard North American plug with two flat parallel pins.

Gambling at Ditch Fridays Pool Party

Embassies

Foreign embassies are all located in Washington, DC. Phone numbers include Britain (tel: 202-588-6500); Germany (tel: 202-298-4000); France (tel: 202-944-6000); and Australia (tel: 202-797-3000). Call directory enquiries (tel: 118) or check www.directoryenquiries.org for the numbers of other embassies.

Emergencies

In case of emergency, call 911. Dial 311 to report a non-emergency incident.

Gambling help

Some people gamble unwisely and get in over their heads, and for them help is just a phone call away. Sponsored jointly by the Nevada Resort Association and the Nevada Council on Problem Gambling, trained counselors stand by 24 hours a day at 800-522-4700, and all calls are confidential. Gamblers Anonymous, a nationwide program for gambling addicts similar to Alcoholics Anonymous, is also active in Las Vegas. There are meetings daily in and around Las Vegas. Their hotline is 888-442-2110 or log on to www.gamblersanonymous.org.

Gaming etiquette

Players must be 21 years or over. No cell phones or electronics are allowed anywhere on the casino floor. Smoking is still permitted in casinos (but largely prohibited elsewhere in the city, see page 117).

Gay and lesbian

The Gay and Lesbian Center (401 South Maryland Parkway; tel: 702-733-9800; www.thecenterlv.com; Mon–Fri 11am–7pm, Sat 10am–3pm) provides plenty of information including a guide to local gay and gay-friendly bars. A number of print publications, available at the Blue Moon Resort, and many other locations around town, help visitors and residents get in touch with Las Vegas's LGBTQ community. The city's original gay underground newspaper, the *Vegas Gay Times*, started publication very secretly in 1979 and later became the *Nevada Gay Times*, then the *Las Vegas Bugle*. Today, no longer underground, it has evolved into *QVegas*, a slick monthly magazine (www.qvegas.com). It is published by VGM LLC (4575 Dean Martin Drive Place; tel: 866-483-4271).

Guided tours

One of the beauties of Las Vegas is that it's an excellent jumping-off point for a remarkable variety of scenic attractions within a day's drive. Most tour operators aim their tours at short-term visitors interested in seeing attractions from the comfort of an air-conditioned bus, Jeep, helicopter, or light aircraft. But you can also find guided tours aimed at outdoors and history buffs, including bicycle tours,

Sculpture outside the Smith Center for the Performing Arts

back-country Jeeping, white-water rafting, and ghost towns.

Guided tours of Hoover Dam, Red Rock Canyon, Lake Mead, Death Valley National Park, the North Rim of Grand Canyon National Park, as well as Zion and Bryce National Parks, are available through reputable tour operators such as Gray Line Bus Tours, Pink Jeep Tours, Papillon Helicopter Tours, Desert Eco Tours, Black Canyon River Adventures, and Escape Adventures/Las Vegas Cyclery, to name a few. Pick-up is usually available at hotels on the Strip.

A handful of tour operators offer tours of Las Vegas itself. Gray Line Bus Tours (tel: 800-472-9546; www.grayline.com) has a nightly six-hour "Neon & Lights" tour, which combines bus ride and walking. A daytime tour takes in Clark County Museum, a history museum.

The 2.5-hour "Haunted Vegas Tour" (tel: 702-677-9015; www.hauntedvegastours.com; 9pm Sat–Thu), based at the Greek Isles Hotel and Resort, combines a cheesy show and guided bus tour to sites such as the Motel of Death (where several celebrities have been murdered), with tales about the restless shades of Bugsy Siegel, Liberace, Elvis, and others.

Vegas Walks (tel: 702-367-1054; www.vegaswalks.com) does historical walking tours of the Strip with guides – a good way to get a handle on Las Vegas's dizzying changes over the last few decades.

Also leisurely is Balloon Las Vegas (4390 Polaris Avenue, Las Vegas; tel: 702-553-3039), which rounds off both its sunrise and sunset flights with a Champagne celebration.

Health

Human beings were not designed to walk around in 100°F (38°C) midday temperatures; hang out in artificially cold, air-conditioned environments; remain seated almost motionless for hours at a time in a casino; eat large quantities of food at an all-you-can-eat buffet; or stay awake for 24 hours at a time. But then the Las Vegas Experience is not the everyday one. It's an extreme blowout of just a few days' duration, for most people. That's what makes it so much fun! In order to keep the fun coming, take the following general precautions, none of which should interfere with having a good time; it should, in fact, prolong it.

Wear a sunblock of 30SPF, sunglasses, a broad-brimmed hat, long-sleeved breathable clothing, and sturdy walking shoes when you walk around outside. Savvy desert residents (including native wildlife) are active outdoors in the early morning, before the sun gets too strong, and in the evenings, after the sun goes down. Your best bet is to stay inside between 2pm and 6pm, the hottest time of day in the desert, perhaps napping, pampering yourself, and/or vis-

Forum shops at Caesar's Palace

iting a museum, then stroll down the Strip and around Downtown for dinner, to catch a show, or see Las Vegas's amazing neon lights.

Keep a one-liter water bottle with you (and keep sipping on it) at all times, to avoid dehydration, and snack on nutritious foods such as salty nuts to maintain an electrolyte balance in the body, especially if you're also drinking strong coffee and alcohol or taking medications, which are very dehydrating. Drinking too much water and eating too little food (hyponutremia) is an underreported danger in the desert, with serious health consequences.

Visitors with fair skin and light-colored eyes should be particularly alert for signs of heat exhaustion (red face, sweating, dizziness), which can come on quickly without you realizing it due to low humidity. Its more serious second stage, heat stroke (pale skin, dizziness, nausea, and lack of sweat), indicates a dangerous overheating of the body core and inability to cool down and should be treated medically, if suspected. To avoid problems, keep the skin and clothing wet (a wet bandana around the neck is an excellent idea) and keep the skin covered to maintain homeostasis in the body. Be careful around the pool. Plunging into cool water when your body has become overheated is inadvisable.

Medical assistance

Walk-in medical clinics are much cheaper than hospital emergency rooms for minor ailments. Foreign visitors are strongly advised to purchase travel insurance before leaving to avoid high urgent-care costs.

University Medical Center (UMC) operates 11 Quick Care clinics in Las Vegas (www.umcsn.com). Two 24-hour medical services are available: 24 Hour Vegas Hotel Doctor (tel: 702-677-2644) and Vegas Quick Care (tel: 702-337-0989). Nearby are the Summerlin Hospital Medical Center (tel: 702-233-7000), Boulder City Hospital (tel: 702-293-4111), and Lake Mead Hospital (tel: 702-657-5512).

Hours and holidays

Las Vegas is a city that never sleeps, and casinos are open 24 hours, every day of the year, as are many service stores, supermarkets, and other businesses. Banks usually keep business hours of 9am to 3pm on weekdays and one evening until 6pm. Post offices are open from 9am to 6pm weekdays and 8am to noon on Saturday.

Public holidays

Public holidays include: New Year's Day (Jan 1); Martin Luther King Day (3rd Monday in Jan); Washington's Birthday (3rd Mon in Feb); Memorial Day (last Mon in May); Independence Day (July 4); Labor Day (1st Mon in Sept); Columbus Day (2nd Mon in Oct); Veterans' Day (Nov 11); Thanksgiving (4th Thu in Nov); and Christmas Day (Dec 25).

Helicopter tour over Grand Canyon West

M

Media

Las Vegas has two daily papers: the *Las Vegas Review Journal* and the *Las Vegas Sun. City Life* and *Las Vegas Weekly* (http://lasvegasweekly.com) are free alternative papers available at many locations. There are seven television stations and 30 radio stations. A traveler's newsletter, the Las Vegas Advisor, offers tips on getting the most out of your Las Vegas trip and is available by subscription from Huntingdon Press (702-252-0655).

What's On (www.ilovevegas.com), a free weekly in-room guide, is a good place to find information about hotel and tour packages.

Casino Player (http://digital.casinoplayer.com) is a trade magazine aimed at serious gamers. For the latest insider information on what's happening in Las Vegas and how to get the most out of your trip, log on to www.lasvegasinsider.com, www.lasvegasadvisor.com, and www.cheapovegas.com.

Outdoor activities

It may seem unlikely but Las Vegas is actually a terrific base for day trips to numerous surrounding outdoor destinations, where you can hike, bike, horseback ride, camp, kayak, waterski, go white-water rafting or speed boating, or just take in incredible desert scenery and history. Water sports such as water-skiing, speed boating, and kayaking are popular on Lake Mead, southeast of Las Vegas.

The best hiking can be found amid the red rocks of Valley of Fire State Park, on the north end of Lake Mead, and Red Rock Canyon National Conservation Area, 30 miles (48km) west of Las Vegas. Around 10 miles (16km) beyond Red Rock Canyon are the Spring Mountains, topped by lofty Mount Charleston, a good place to camp as well as hike and escape desert heat in summer and enjoy snow sports in winter.

Farther afield, Grand Canyon, Zion, Bryce Canyon, Joshua Tree, and Death Valley national parks are renowned for their extraordinary scenery and outdoor activities. Hoover Dam is a must-see for its historic importance as well as the sheer scope of its engineering.

Post

The Downtown post office is located at 201 Las Vegas Boulevard South, Site 100, and is open Monday to Friday 8.30am to 5pm. The post office at the airport is open Monday to Friday 9am to 1pm and 2pm to 5pm.

Effective first-class domestic postage rates are 47 cents for the first ounce (28g) with 21 cents for each additional ounce. Postcards are 34 cents each.

Pool party

S

Smoking

In keeping with the Sin City approach to life of "anything goes," smoking is very common in Las Vegas, especially on the casino floor. Smoking is not permitted in restaurants, bars serving food, at the airport, or the convention center. Hotels offer non-smoking rooms, but if you are sensitive to cigarette smoke, choose one that is entirely non-smoking and patronize establishments with clear non-smoking policies.

T

Telephones

The area code for Las Vegas is 702. Local calls are free (although some hotels impose an access charge for in-room calls). Calls from a coin box will require change, a credit card, or calling card available at many supermarkets. Some callboxes offer Internet access by the minute. For local information, dial 411.

Tickets

The sheer number of shows and concerts in Las Vegas is staggering. There's something here for everyone, from the Folies Bergère to lounge acts, the cerebral antics of the Blue Men, or concerts by headliners such as Elton John and Celine Dion. Tickets usually go on sale three months in advance for the most popular shows. For the best seats, call the day these go on sale – they sell out very fast – and expect to pay $150–$220 per person.

If an event is sold out, you may be able to get tickets (at super-premium prices) through a reputable online broker such as www.tickco.com. Avoid buying tickets through eBay and other auction sites, as fraud is rife. High-rollers in the casinos are often given complimentary premium show tickets as an added incentive, so if you want Las Vegas at your feet, win big.

Time differences

Most of Nevada is in the Pacific Time Zone: two hours behind Chicago, three hours behind New York, and eight hours behind London.

Tipping

Tipping (often called 'tokes' in Las Vegas) is the grease that keeps the machine of Las Vegas operating, far more than in other American cities.

Most tipping is in the $2–5 range, but sometimes a larger tip will help things move along. No table available at a big hotel restaurant for hours? A $10 or $20 bill will usually get you a seat immediately. Valet parking full? Try $5 first, more if it is a holiday or special event, and a space will often magically appear. If at valet pick-up a huge group of people are already waiting for their cars, waits of up to 20 minutes are not uncommon; however, a bill with the right picture on it handed to

Cabanas line the swimming pool at the Hard Rock Hotel

the ticket taker with a request to speed up the process will almost always have you out pretty quickly. When you tip under these circumstances, do so discreetly.

Restaurant tipping ranges between 15 to 20 percent of the total bill before taxes. A good tipper will go to 25 percent for extraordinary service. Be warned: some restaurants automatically include a 15 percent surcharge for large tables; you may argue the charge if service is poor. If it is included, you may of course add a small percentage for exceptional service. Remember, if service is bad, you are not obligated to tip, but select another server the next time you visit that establishment.

Here are some general suggestions for how much to tip, but when in doubt, always overtip: in Las Vegas, this may improve your vacation immeasurably:
Bartenders: $1–2 per round for two or more
Bellmen: $1–2 per bag
Cocktail Waitresses: $1–2 per round
Concierges: $5 and up, depending on service
Doormen: $1 per bag, $1 for cab call
Limo Drivers: 15 percent of total bill
Maids: $2 per day, left at the end of stay
Pool Attendants: $1
Taxi Drivers: 20 percent
Valet Parking: $2 when car is returned; $5–10 to find a spot on a busy night; $5 to ticket taker for fast return
Wait Staff (Restaurant): 15–20 percent of total before taxes
Wait Staff (Showroom): $5–10

Tipping in Casinos
Change Attendants: 5 percent and up, depending on your luck and their interaction.
Cocktail Waitresses: $1, particularly if the drink is free; tipping with gaming chips is acceptable as well.
Dealers: If you are winning, tip the dealer by placing a bet for him or her, one-half of your bet; when leaving the table in the black, tip according to your conscience.

Tourist information

The main one-stop shop for information is Las Vegas Convention and Visitors Authority (3150 Paradise Road (corner of Desert Inn Road); tel: 702-892-7575; toll free 877-847-4858), which has specialized information on everything from getting married to facilities for disabled travelers to visiting with kids.

LVCVA has tourist information offices abroad to help you plan your trip. On the web, look up www.lasvegasfreedom, plus the suffix for your country (www.lasvegasfreedom.co.uk for the UK, for example). Other good sites include www.vegas.com for attractions, and www.lvchamber.com for events and local news.

The State of Nevada Welcome Centers (www.travelnevada.com) also offer good information, if you're driv-

McCarran International Airport

ing to Las Vegas. There are Welcome Centers at Mesquite, near the Utah state line, and Primm, near the California state line.

Transportation

Airports and arrival

Most people fly or drive to Las Vegas or arrive by Greyhound bus. There is no longer any rail service to the city. Vegas is served by McCarran International Airport (http://mccarran.com), 1 mile (2km) from the Strip and 5 miles (8km) from Downtown. One of the 12 busiest airports in the world, it has 1,100 flights daily via 40 different carriers and direct connections to 125 US cities. The most economical way to reach your hotel is by 24-hour shuttle; fares to the Strip and Downtown are less than $20. Taxi fares start at $3.70, with $2.80 per mile (2km) thereafter.

Car rental

All the major car rental companies have kiosks at the airport; rates begin at $35–40 per day. You must be 21 or over (25 at some locations) to rent a car and have a valid driver's license and at least one major credit card. Air-conditioning is vital, if you don't want to cook inside your vehicle. Dream Car Rentals (tel: 877-707-8342) and Gotham Dream Cars (tel: 877-246-8426) specialize in exotic cars. Eaglerider (tel: 702-876-8687) rents motorcycles.

Las Vegas has wide boulevards, and getting around by car is easy. Parking isn't allowed on the Strip: use free valet parking at hotel casinos and then tip the valet a couple of bucks.

Driving

The main route through Las Vegas is Interstate 15 (I-15) from Los Angeles, California, a four-hour drive away, substantially longer when traffic is heavy on holiday weekends. I-15 continues north, through scenic Virgin River Gorge to Saint George, Utah, a good jumping-off point for national parks including Zion, Bryce, and the Grand Canyon. I-15 continues north to the state capital of Salt Lake City. If you're driving from Phoenix, Arizona, take Highway 93 north via I-40 and Hoover Dam to Las Vegas.

A word of caution: If you plan on driving through the desert, be sure to carry a good map, a spare tire, extra water – at least a gallon (4 liters) per person per day to avoid dehydration – nutritious snacks, and let someone know where you are going. A cell phone is a good idea but may not work in some areas; the same is true for GPS units powered by satellite.

Service stations may be few and far between outside Las Vegas; fill up when you can. If your car breaks down on a back road, don't attempt to strike out on foot, even with water. A car is easier to spot than a person and provides shelter from the elements. Sit tight and wait to be found.

Las Vegas Monorail

Public transportation

Public bus transportation is operated by Citizens Area Transit (CAT). There are numerous bus routes throughout the area; a one-way fare on the Strip costs $4, and slightly less in the rest of the city. Buses on the Strip run 24 hours a day, seven days a week. For the latest information and scheduling, call cat-ride (tel: 702-228-7433; www.rtcsouthernnevada.com). A trolley runs the length of the Strip 9.30am to 1.30am. Reasonable fares and good-value day passes are available.

The privately funded Las Vegas Monorail (Mon–Thu 7am–2am, Fri–Sun 7am–3am) travels along the east side of the Strip behind the resorts, from the SLS Hotel to the MGM Grand, with the following stops in between: Las Vegas Hilton, Las Vegas Convention Center, Harrah's/The Linq, the Flamingo/Caesars Palace, and Bally's/Paris.

Visas and passports

Foreign travelers to the US (including those from Mexico) must carry a valid passport and a short-term visa, known as an ESTA. For those who are planning on visiting for more than 90 days, a different visa is required. Regulations are frequently subject to change so for the most current information, contact the US Department of Homeland Security at www.dhs.gov.

W

Websites and Internet cafés

Log on to the Las Vegas Convention and Visitors Authority website (www.lvcva.com/) to plan your trip. Other websites are noted in "Tourist information" (see page 118).

Almost every single hotel and hostel offers Wi-Fi. If they don't, then you need to change accommodations because you've accidently gone back in time and booked into a cave. Some will be free, others will be charged. Chances are, the big hotels on the Strip will charge and the cheaper motels won't. There are also a number of free hot spots all around the place, like any one of the many, many Starbucks coffee shops; most bars provide free Wi-Fi and even some shops. All you have to do is ask.

If you do not have a computer but want to check your email or surf the Internet, check out one of the local Internet cafés. They include Pride Factory (Suite E-1B, Commercial Center, 953 East Sahara Avenue; tel: 702-444-1291; www.pridefactory.com; daily 10am–midnight) and Elysium Internet Cafe (7875 West Sahara Avenue, #101; tel: 702-307-4931; daily, 24 hours).

Although very expensive to use, there are branches of FedEx's between the Strip and the convention center (tel: 702-951-2400; daily 24 hours), near

Driving into Las Vegas

the UNLV campus (tel: 702-735-4402; daily 7am–midnight), and near Downtown (tel: 702-383-7022; daily 7am–11pm). They each have a T-Mobile Wi-Fi Hotspot.

Weddings

With its easy-to-obtain marriage licenses and thousands of over-the-top nuptial options, Las Vegas is the wedding capital of the world. Neither blood tests nor waiting periods are required if you want to tie the knot. The legal age is 18 for both men and women (proof of age is required) and licensing fees are $60. Civil ceremonies can be performed at the Marriage Commissioner's Office at 309 South 3rd Street Chapel; fees vary depending on the services provided. For marriage license information contact the Clark County Marriage License Bureau (201 Clark Avenue; located on the northwest corner of Clark Avenue and 3rd Street; tel: 702-671-0600; daily 8am–midnight, including holidays).

Same-sex marriages aren't recognized in Nevada but same-sex commitment ceremonies can be arranged through gay-owned Viva Las Vegas Villas & Wedding Chapel (800-574-4450; www.vivalasvegasweddings.com).

You can get married in Vegas even if you're not a US resident. To recognize the union legally, most countries require a certified copy of your marriage certificate ($10) and an apostille from the Nevada Secretary of State ($20). Contact your home country's consulate office in Washington, DC, to inquire if additional certifications are required.

Weights and measures

Despite efforts to convert to metric, the US still uses the Imperial system of weights and measures. However, note that the US gallon is approximately 16 percent smaller than the standard Imperial gallon.

Women

Like New Orleans, Las Vegas is unabashedly a party town, where you are encouraged to act out on your fantasies, lubricated by large quantities of low-cost alcoholic drinks and a permissive attitude enshrined in Vegas's marketing theme: "What happens in Vegas, stays in Vegas." For women, this can be a mixed bag. In such an atmosphere, men are encouraged to view women as objects for their pleasure, and the old stereotype of the high-roller and his beautiful call girl is still very much a part of the scene, even though prostitution is officially illegal.

However, that said, in these modern times you'll find just as many groups of girls doing exactly the same thing as groups of guys are doing. If you're a solo woman, you'll find plenty of flirting in Las Vegas's burgeoning club scene. Unfortunately, you may also receive some harassment by obnoxious drunken young men. Without a doubt, there's safety in numbers.

Casino

BOOKS AND FILM

Films

Las Vegas has long since provided an exciting location to set stories and also to incorporate plots around. Within this oasis of opulence, fortunes have been made and squandered in the blink of an eye and the bright neon backdrop of the Strip has kept Sin City in the movies and in the business of movies. The fact that Hollywood is just five hours' drive away also helps.

The original *Ocean's 11*, made in 1960, was the famous Rat Pack saga, directed by Lewis Milestone and shot when Frank Sinatra, Dean Martin, Sammy Davis Jr, and Peter Lawford could spare time from carousing. The film was remade in 2001 with George Clooney, Brad Pitt, Matt Damon, and Julia Roberts topping a stellar bill, and features several scenes filmed in the Bellagio. Elvis Presley wooed Ann-Margret from the Sahara on the Strip all the way to Lake Mead and Mount Charleston in *Viva Las Vegas* (1964); the famous pairing was rumored to be mirrored off screen. In 1971 Sean Connery went Downtown to Fremont Street as James Bond in *Diamonds Are Forever*.

The Mafia has received a lot of attention in the cinema. In 1972 and 1974, parts 1 and 2 of Francis Ford Coppola's *The Godfather* trilogy were partly filmed and set locally. The saga of the Corleone family includes references to the Mob's attempts at legitimacy in the Nevada gaming business. Warren Beatty played a highly romanticized Benjamin "Bugsy" Siegel while conducting an on-screen romance with his soon-to-be wife Annette Bening in Barry Levinson's Bugsy in 1991. Martin Scorsese's *Casino* (1995), starring Robert de Niro and Sharon Stone, is a brutally epic tale of mobsters hustling their way into the casino business, much of it filmed in the Strip's Riviera casino.

Vegas has served as the backdrop for cheesy sci-fi movies as well. In *The Amazing Colossal Man* (1957) Las Vegas came under attack from an Army officer who grew 60ft (18 meters) tall after surviving an atomic explosion, but the assault came from elsewhere in Tim Burton's wild 1996 sci-fi fantasy, *Mars Attacks*, in which the Strip was spectacularly demolished.

Dustin Hoffman won an Oscar for his role in *Rain Man* in 1988, which co-starred Tom Cruise and featured a scene filmed in the Pompeii-style Fantasy Suite of Caesars Palace.

Johnny Depp took narcotics aplenty and trashed a hotel room as a reporter covering a Mint 400 motorbike race in the 1998 film of Hunter S. Thompson's *Fear and Loathing in Las Vegas*, filmed partly in the Riviera, Circus Circus, and Stardust hotels. Nicolas Cage is a virtual Vegas veteran, having starred in

Fear and Loathing in Las Vegas

several local movies: the 1992 comedy *Honeymoon in Vegas* that features the Bally's Casino Resort and the Excalibur; the dark 1995 drama *Leaving Las Vegas*; two years later, *Con Air*; and the following year, *Snake Eyes*. In 2007 he starred as a Vegas-based clairvoyant in the movie *Next*.

Vince Vaughn and Jon Favreau spent a night womanizing in Vegas – specifically, outside the Stardust and inside the Fremont Hotel and Casino – in the 1996 epic romantic comedy *Swingers*. Favreau returned to the scene in 1998 with the much darker *Very Bad Things*, on the worst that can happen in Vegas.

It was the 2001 remake of *Ocean's Eleven* that really unleashed a rush of interest in using Las Vegas as the glamorous backdrop to a number of films and television programs. Since then, William H. Macy played the unluckiest man alive in *The Cooler*, a gritty, violent, yet charming meditation on the nature of luck in old-time Vegas. Alec Baldwin was also nominated for both an Oscar and a Golden Globe for Best Supporting Actor in 2004 for his role in the film.

Then in 2009, *The Hangover* set a new standard in comedy and portrayed Vegas as a magnet for misbehavior, overflowing with opportunities for indulgence. The movie itself was filmed all over Vegas.

Books

Sin City has also featured prominently in literature, including the legendary novel *Fear and Loathing in Las Vegas* by Hunter S. Thompson about an eccentric journalist and his lawyer who travel to the Las Vegas of the psychedelic 1960s, and *Literary Las Vegas: The Best Writing About America's Most Fabulous City*, an eclectic compendium of writers on Las Vegas that includes Tom Wolfe's famous essay from *The Kandy-Kolored Tangerine-Flake Streamline Baby*, his first collected book of essays.

The Nevadan art historian and Vegas resident Dave Hickey has written a fascinating memoir entitled *Air Guitar: Essays on Art & Democracy* and of course John O'Brien wrote *Leaving Las Vegas*, the searing novel of alcohol, obsession, and suicide that became an award-winning film starring Nicholas Cage.

Now seen as a bible for postmodernist architecture, Robert Venturi, Denise Scott Brown, and Steven Izenour's book, *Learning from Las Vegas: The Forgotten Symbolism of Architectural Form* is a seminal book that describes the urban sprawl of Las Vegas as an architecture of communication over space, achieved through style and signs.

The Delivery Man by Joe McGinniss Jr is an electric debut novel about Generation Y, set against the real lives and suburbs and gated communities of today's Las Vegas.

The Desert Rose by Pulitzer-prize winning author Larry McMurtry is a compelling story of Harmony, an ageing Las Vegas showgirl, in a novel that is both tough and tender.

ABOUT THIS BOOK

This *Explore Guide* has been produced by the editors of Insight Guides, whose books have set the standard for visual travel guides since 1970. With top-quality photography and authoritative recommendations, these guidebooks bring you the very best routes and itineraries in the world's most exciting destinations.

BEST ROUTES

The routes in the book provide something to suit all budgets, tastes and trip lengths. As well as covering the destination's many classic attractions, the itineraries track lesser-known sights, and there are also excursions for those who want to extend their visit outside the city. The routes embrace a range of interests, so whether you are an art fan, a gourmet, a history buff or have kids to entertain, you will find an option to suit.

We recommend reading the whole of a route before setting out. This should help you to familiarise yourself with it and enable you to plan where to stop for refreshments – options are shown in the 'Food and Drink' box at the end of each tour.

For our pick of the tours by theme, consult Recommended Routes for... (see pages 6–7).

INTRODUCTION

The routes are set in context by this introductory section, giving an overview of the destination to set the scene, plus background information on food and drink, shopping and more, while a succinct history timeline highlights the key events over the centuries.

DIRECTORY

Also supporting the routes is a Directory chapter, with a clearly organised A–Z of practical information, our pick of where to stay while you are there and select restaurant listings; these eateries complement the more low-key cafés and restaurants that feature within the routes and are intended to offer a wider choice for evening dining. Also included here are some nightlife listings and our recommendations for books and films about the destination.

ABOUT THE AUTHOR

Having received his training on Fleet Street in the UK, Scott Snowden has been a travel journalist for nearly 20 years. He has written for the likes of *Time Out*, *The Sunday Times*, *Travel Weekly* and numerous other newspapers and magazines. Scott has also worked for CNN and was also editor-in-chief of the successful UK magazine *Total Travel*. Scott first found himself in Vegas for work-related conventions. Paying little more than minor attention to his surroundings, it seemed every conference and expo that he had to attend was held there. In an effort to save his sanity, he began searching for something other than the Strip and unexpectedly discovered a wealth of history and culture. Before long, he was leaving all his colleagues behind to entertain themselves in the big casino resorts up and down the Strip and was exploring all the other sights and venues. These days, he finds any reason he possibly can to return to the so-called Sin City and will happily talk for hours about how interesting it actually is to anyone that will listen.

CONTACT THE EDITORS

We hope you find this Explore Guide useful, interesting and a pleasure to read. If you have any questions or feedback on the text, pictures or maps, please do let us know. If you have noticed any errors or outdated facts, or have suggestions for places to include on the routes, we would be delighted to hear from you. Please drop us an email at hello@insightguides.com. Thanks!

CREDITS

Explore Las Vegas
Editor: Tom Fleming
Author: Scott Snowden
Head of Production: Rebeka Davies
Picture Editor: Tom Smyth
Cartography: original cartography Apa Cartography Department, updated by Carte
Photo credits: Al Argueta/Apa Publications 8ML, 8MC, 10B, 12, 13M, 13T, 12/13T, 14B, 15, 23L, 26ML, 26MC, 26ML, 44, 44/45, 47, 60, 74T, 75L, 74/75, 76/77, 81L, 80/81, 92, 110, 111, 112, 113, 114, 115, 116, 117, 118, 119, 120, 121; Alamy 7MR, 32, 38, 48, 48/49, 50, 52, 122, 123; Caesars Entertainment 4ML, 8MC, 8MR, 14T, 16, 71, 82MC, 82MC, 82/83T, 87, 91, 104/105; Carol M. Highsmith/LOC 4ML, 26MC, 82ML; Cirque du Soleil 55; Denise Truscello/Caesars Entertainment 104; Denise Truscello/MGM Resorts International 107; Douglas Friedman/ MGM Resorts International 4MC; Erik Kabik/ erikkabik.com 51; FLPA 7M, 32/33; Getty Images 1, 4/5T, 6MC, 8/9T, 10/11T, 17L, 20, 21L, 20/21, 24, 25, 26/27T, 28/29, 33L, 34/35, 36, 39L, 49L, 53, 54, 73L; Heart Attack Grill 101; Hilton Hotels & Resorts 56; iStock 7T, 7MR, 8MR, 19M, 26MR, 30, 72, 78, 79, 80; Ken Lund 62/63; Leonardo 82ML, 85, 94, 95; Mars, Inc 57, 58B; MGM Resorts International 4MR, 59, 82MR, 82MR, 84, 86, 88, 89, 90, 93, 96, 97, 98, 99, 100, 105L, 106, 109; Nevada State Museum 62; Nowitz Photography/Apa Publications 4MR, 6BC, 16/17, 18, 19T, 18/19T, 22, 22/23, 26MR, 42, 43L, 42/43, 45L, 46, 61, 63L, 65, 66B, 66T, 67, 68, 69L, 68/69, 70, 72/73; Pizza Rock Las Vegas 103; Press Association Images 37, 58T; Public domain 74B; Richard Faverty/TRP Entertainment, LLC 31; Shutterstock 38/39; South Point Hotel and Casino 102; Sydney Martinez/TravelNevada 64; Thomas Gensinger/Dig This 6ML; Tomasz Rossa/Wynn 41; Wynn 4MC, 6TL, 8ML, 40, 108
Cover credits: Shutterstock (main) iStock (bottom)

Printed by CTPS – China

First Edition 2017

DISTRIBUTION

UK, Ireland and Europe
Apa Publications (UK) Ltd
sales@insightguides.com
United States and Canada
Ingram Publisher Services
ips@ingramcontent.com
Australia and New Zealand
Woodslane
info@woodslane.com.au
Southeast Asia
Apa Publications (Singapore) Pte
singaporeoffice@insightguides.com
Hong Kong, Taiwan and China
Apa Publications (HK) Ltd
hongkongoffice@insightguides.com
Worldwide
Apa Publications (UK) Ltd
sales@insightguides.com

SPECIAL SALES, CONTENT LICENSING AND COPUBLISHING

Insight Guides can be purchased in bulk quantities at discounted prices. We can create special editions, personalised jackets and corporate imprints tailored to your needs.
sales@insightguides.com
www.insightguides.biz

INDEX

18b Arts District **38**

A

Adventuredome **48**
age restrictions **110**
airports and arrival **119**
aquarium **32**
Arts Factory **38**
Atlatl Rock **78**

B

Bally's **44**
Barrick Museum **38**
Bellagio **39, 45, 74**
  Conservatory and Botanical Gardens **45**
  Gallery of Fine Art **39**
Big Shot **54**
Bill's **44**
blackjack **20, 68**
books **123**
Boulder City **81**
budgeting **110**

C

Caesars Palace **44, 65**
car rental **119**
childcare **111**
children **110**
Chinatown **45**
Circus Circus **48, 73**
Cirque du Soleil **40, 46, 55, 59**
  Zumanity **59**
climate **14, 111**
clothing **111**
Contemporary Arts Collective **39**
Cowboy Trail Rides **63**
craps **20, 67**
crime and safety **111**
currency and taxes **112**
customs **112**

D

Dig This **54**
disabled travelers **112**
Downtown **13, 28**
driving **119**
Dust Gallery **39**

E

electricity **112**
embassies **113**
emergencies **113**
Ethel M's Chocolate Factory and Botanical Gardens **58**
Excalibur **46, 51, 58**

F

films **122**
First Friday **38**
Flamingo **30, 44, 74**
Flamingo Las Vegas **34**
Floyd Lamb State Park **62**
Flyaway Indoor Skydiving **52**
food and drink **16**
Forum Shops **44**
Fremont Street **28, 75**
Fremont Street Experience (Viva Vision) **75**

G

gambling **20, 65**
gambling help **113**
gaming etiquette **113**
Garden of the Gods **70**
gay and lesbian **113**
Godt-Cleary Arts **39**
Golden Gate Hotel **60**
gondola ride **50**
Grand Canal Shoppes **36, 44**
Grand Canyon West **80**
Greek Isles Hotel **31**
guided tours **113**

H

health **114**
Henderson **76**
Hilton **56**
history **24**
Hoover Dam **79**
hotels
  Artisan Hotel **91**
  Bally's Las Vegas **85**
  Bellagio **86**
  Caesars Palace **86**
  Circus Circus Hotel, Theme Park, and Casino **84**
  Comfort Inn & Suites **91**
  Delano Las Vegas **87**
  Encore **87**
  Excalibur **88**
  Flamingo Las Vegas **88**
  Four Seasons Hotel **88**
  Golden Gate Hotel **92**
  Hard Rock Hotel and Casino **92**
  Harrah's **88**
  Hilton Lake Las Vegas Resort and Casino **92**
  Hooters Casino Hotel **92**
  Luxor **89**
  Mandalay Bay Resort and Casino **89**
  MGM Grand **89**
  Monte Carlo **90**
  Motel 6 **93**
  Motel 8 Las Vegas **90**
  New York New York **90**
  Palace Station Hotel and Casino **93**
  Paris Las Vegas **91**
  Red Rock Casino Resort and Spa **93**
  SLS Las Vegas **84**
  The Cosmopolitan of Las Vegas **86**
  The Cromwell Las Vegas Hotel & Casino **86**
  The LINQ 88
  The Mirage **84**
  The Palazzo **90**
  Treasure Island **84**
  Tropicana Resort and Casino **91**

Vdara Hotel and Spa **93**
Venetian Resort, Hotel, and Casino **85**
Wynn Las Vegas **85**
hours and holidays **115**
Hualapai Ranch **80**

I

Insanity **54**

K

keno **21**

L

Lake Las Vegas **57**
Lake Mead **76**
Larry's Hideaway **64**
Las Vegas Natural History Museum **46, 63**
Le Rêve **40**
Linq **44, 74**
Lion Habitat Ranch **34**
Lost City Museum **78**
Luxor **46, 75**

M

Madame Tussaud's **50**
Madame Tussauds **44**
magicians **50**
Mandalay Bay **46, 58**
Mandalay Bay Hotel **35**
Manhattan Express **55**
Marjorie Barrick Museum **33**
media **116**
MGM Grand **50, 55, 74**
mini-baccarat **70**
Mirage **32, 44, 73**
monorail **54**
Monte Carlo **45**
Mouse's Tank **78**

N

National Finals Rodeo **62**
Neon Museum **37**
Nevada State Museum and Historical Society **62**
New York New York **45, 55, 58, 59, 74**
nightlife **104**
Northshore Road **77**

O

Old Las Vegas Mormon Fort State Park **60**
outdoor activities **116**

P

Paris Las Vegas **43, 74**
people **14**
poker **21, 69**
post **116**
public holidays **115**
public transportation **120**

R

race book **68**
Red Square **58**
Regis Galerie **36**
restaurants
Andiron Steak & Sea **100**
Andre's **97**
AquaKnox **94**
Aureole **97**
Battista's Hole in the Wall **31**
Border Grill **98**
Bouchon **41, 94**
Carbone **98**
Carson Kitchen **100**
Charlie Palmer Steakhouse **98**
Chengdu Taste **101**
Chow **101**
Circus Buffet **51**
Craftsteak **98**
Cravings **35**
Crush **98**
CUT Las Vegas **94**
Delmonico's Steakhouse **94**
Eat **101**
Eiffel Tower Restaurant **99**
Emeril's New Orleans Fish House **55**
Fix **99**
Golden Steer Steakhouse **101**
Harley-Davidson Café **44**
Hash House A Go Go **95**
Heart Attack Grill **75, 101**
Hofbräuhaus **47**
Hugo's Cellar **102**
Javier's **99**
Jimmy Buffet's Margaritaville **44**
Joe's Seafood Prime Steak and Stone Crab **95**
L'Atelier de Joel Robuchon **97**
Lawry's The Prime Rib **102**
Le Village Buffet **47**
Lotus of Siam **102**
Michael Mina **99**
Michael's Gourmet Room **102**
Mizumi **47**
Nora's Italian Cuisine **102**
Old Homestead Steakhouse **71**
Origin India **41**
Palm Restaurant **95**
Pamplemousse **103**
Paradise Café **35**
Peppermill Inn **31**
Picasso **41, 99**
Pizza Rock **103**
Poolside Bar & Grill **59**
Portofino **96**
Prime Steakhouse **100**
Rainforest Café **35, 50**
Raku **103**
Roy's Las Vegas **103**
Sid's Café **51**
Spago **71, 100**
SW Steakhouse **96**
Therapy **103**

Tiffany's Café **31**
Top of the World **96**
Top of the World Restaurant **59**
Veggie House **35**
Wicked Spoon Buffet **100**
Wynn Buffet **41**
Yardbird Southern Table & Bar **96**
Yard House **75, 96**
restaurantsCafé Americano **71**
restaurantsDu-Par's Restaurant & Bakery **64**
Rogers Warm Spring **77**
roulette **21, 68**

S

S2 Art Group **38**
Shark Reef **35**
shopping **18**
Siegfried and Roy's Secret Garden and Dolphin Habitat **33**
skydiving **53**
Skywalk **80**
slot machines **66**
Slots-A-Fun **72**
SLS Hotel & Casino **72**
smoking **117**
sports book **68**
Spring Mountain Ranch **63**
Stratosphere Tower **54**
Strip, the **10**

T

telephones **117**
tickets **117**
time differences **117**
tipping **117**
tourist information **118**
Tournament of Kings **51**
transportation **119**

U

UNLV Arboretum **34**

V

Valley of Fire State Park **78**
Venetian **36, 44, 50, 73**
video poker **67**
visas and passports **120**

W

websites and Internet cafés **120**
weddings **22, 121**
weights and measures **121**
Westgate Las Vegas Resort & Casino **50**
women **121**
Wynn Las Vegas **40**

X

X Scream **54**

Z

Zoo **34**

MAP LEGEND

Start of tour
Tour & route direction
Recommended sight
Recommended restaurant/café
Tourist information
Railway
Monorail
Place of interest
Main post office
Main bus station
Summit
Park
Important building
Hotel
Transport hub
Shop / market
Urban area
National park